PRAISE FOR SUSAN CHERNAK MCELROY

Heart in the Wild

"An unforgettable journey of self-disc... shares poetic and true-to-the-bone insights into the natural world's laws, including that human lives—like those of the animal kingdom—must endure destruction and dormancy, but that ultimately a season of new growth arrives."
—*Healing Retreats & Spa* magazine

"Powerful . . . On nearly every page, McElroy discovers new insight."
—*Jackson Hole News*

"An inspirational memoir."
—*Publishers Weekly*

Animals as Teachers and Healers

"Filled with parables of a delicate, philosophical nature."
—*Los Angeles Times*

"A treat for anyone who cares about animals or secretly thinks they might be angels in disguise."
—*New Age Journal*

Animals as Guides for the Soul

"Passionate . . . Captivating . . . The result is a psychological salve."
—*The Seattle Times*

"Open, honest, and generous, Susan Chernak McElroy reveals the possibilities of magical encounters and surprising connections with animals in daily life."
—DEENA METZGER, author of *Writing for Your Life*

BY SUSAN CHERNAK McELROY

Animals as Teachers and Healers

Animals as Guides for the Soul:
Stories of Life-Changing Encounters

Heart in the Wild: A Journey of
Self-Discovery with Animals of the Wilderness

Heart

in the

Wild

A Journey of Self-Discovery

with Animals of the Wilderness

Susan Chernak McElroy

ILLUSTRATIONS BY CONNIE BOWEN

BALLANTINE BOOKS · NEW YORK

A Ballantine Book
Published by The Random House Publishing Group
Copyright © 2002 by Susan Chernak McElroy
Illustrations copyright © 2002 by Connie Bowen

www.ballantinebooks.com

Library of Congress Control Number: 2003096649

ISBN 0-345-44287-3

Text design by Ann Gold
Cover design by Richard Rossiter
Cover photo © Ron Watts/CORBIS

Manufactured in the United States of America

First Edition: July 2002
First Trade Paperback Edition: December 2003

10   9   8   7   6   5   4   3   2   1

Dedicated to my cherished teachers:
David Bearclaw Abrams,
Elk,
and All My Relations
(Mitaku Oyasin)

My barn having burned to the ground,
I can now see the moon.

—*Anonymous*

Contents

Acknowledgments

Books are so much a group process that I would be foolish to call these works "mine." I have been carried all along the way in my writing work by many, many hands. And so thank you to the gifted, the generous, the supportive, the mysterious, the loyal, and all the rest of my extended family who have helped me and continue to help me in my writing and in my life:

Thank you, David Bearclaw Abrams and Star Abrams, for so many comforting afternoons and evenings in the cabin, for too much good food, and never too much good conversation.

Thank you to my wonderful Wyoming women friends, Janet and Meredith Woodland, Teresa Jackson, and Gael Summer. Janet, if anyone embodies the gifts of the clan mother, Loves All Things, it is most certainly you. Teresa, I hold treasured memories of precious ceremonies together: the making of my medicine wheel, the blessings of both our houses, and so many others. More than anyone I know, you have taught me about the true grace of the quiet healer. Gael, you gave meaning to the words *dream master* and have been a heartfelt champion of my humble efforts at manifesting my own dreams. Meredith, to you I owe my hope for the youth of the world. You are magnificent, womanly, and wise at only nineteen. In your arms rests the saving of the world, and Earth Mother is certainly in good hands there.

Thank you, Leslie Meredith and Tracy Brown, my Ballantine editors, for taking my words and making them clearer and cleaner. And many thanks, Connie Bowen, for your delicate drawings, which add such a lovely visual element to a story that has lived, until now, in my inner vision alone.

Thank you, Lee McElroy, for our continued warm friendship, forged amid a cultural and personal hailstorm. You have shown me over and over again that divorce does not have to mean the death of relationship—only its transformation.

Thank you to my Sun Dance brothers and sisters and my Corn Dance family. All these extended relatives prove to me that we are never limited to family of blood and birthright alone.

Thank you to Creator, to the good spirits of the four directions, to the winged ones, the swimmers, the stands tall people, the stone people, the four-leggeds and two-leggeds, the six- and eight-leggeds. Thank you, spirits of wind, water, and fire. Thank you, Arrow and Strongheart and Mirella and Flora. And thank you, Mother of us all—Earth—for love and abundance without end.

Last, thank you, thank you, Fritz Saam. Your enduring gifts of devotion, radical dialogue, and love for me and for the printed word have done so much to bring this book—and my life—to light. Someday I'll help you to tell your own story of solitude, travel, and healing. Yes, it's true!

Introduction

Give Us Burning

Truth is fire, and to speak the truth means to illuminate and burn.
—L. Schefer

This book is about wild animals, wild forces, and what the wild has to teach us of the humbling—yet renewing—seasons of change and transition in our lives. It is about wild fears, and wildfires—physical and metaphoric ones. It is about the fires of the year 2000—the ones that burned the West and the one that took my home in January of that year.

My catastrophic house fire was not the first fire to have touched my life. If you imagine fire not in its flaming form but as a transitional force that sweeps in, consuming and transmuting all it touches, then the soul of fire had certainly entered me before. None of us is immune to the spirit of fire that rushes upon us, signaling profound and deep life changes with a terrifying rush of obliterating smoke that blackens out the meaning and oftentimes the very sense of reality of our former lives.

Some of us are fighting multiple blazes at once: divorce, job loss, moves, deaths, illness, lost dreams. Some of us face just one massive firestorm at a time. But all of us have had— or will have—our feet to the flames. Twelve years before the fire that consumed my house, my firestorm had been cancer—an advanced stage of malignancy in my neck that had spread to my lymph nodes. At the time of diagnosis, I was only thirty-seven years old.

Endings, fallow times, new beginnings. In every transitional challenge in my life, whether the fires I faced were voluntary or seemed forced upon me, these three tasks marked the ambiguous pathway of personal renewal and integration that change demands. Each fire was an initiation master, a wise teacher, signaling the end of life as I had known it. Each fire burned my life to the ground in large or small ways, changing the look and feel of my inner forest floor. Each fire burned deep enough to usher in a season of spiritual winter, in which all of my life rested quiet and seemingly dead beneath the ash of my former existence and the green shoots of rebirth and fresh beginnings slept under the charred foundation of my life, unseen.

Few of us are courageous enough to welcome endings, to explore them with the focus and attention they deserve. Rather, we celebrate endings simply as beginnings and brush aside the necessary grief work and reflection endings ask of us. Abrupt endings that seem forced upon us—such as the end of my illusion of health after cancer struck or the destruction of my house by fire, which came swiftly and without warning—bring a wave of numbness on their heels, making it easier to avoid looking them close in the face. But to avoid engagement with our endings is to block our ears to a voice that has much to offer us, even as we turn our faces too eagerly toward a new beginning. What have we ended? What have we lost? What has this ending cost our hearts, our lives, our hope in life?

If facing endings takes a brave soul, far braver yet is the person who can sit faithfully between an ending and a new beginning and not try with everything in his or her power to hurry the uncomfortable disengagement process along. There is a time after a wildfire when the ground seems to just sit and hold its breath. Here in the West, the fires of 2000 were only fully ended when the winter snows came. The land went from black to white, and for six months it looked as if nothing were happening. But beneath the snow, and deeper still, beneath the scorched ground, change was moving forward resolutely, undeniably. In accordance with a process as mysterious, enduring, and unstoppable as our own life changes, powerful, unnameable forces were remapping the vision of the forest to come. But the regrowth would not begin instantly or at the surface level.

And so it is with our own changes as well. Fallow time, the time of free-floating discomfort between the end of one way of life and the beginning of the next, is a time when change is occurring on the deepest level, below the ground of our conscious awareness. We rush this time at our peril. For new growth to be genuine and enduring, the ground must be well prepared, and that preparation takes time.

In the end, with or without my faith that they would ever come, new beginnings sprang from the destruction of my old life. This is the universal truth of fire, which is why fire is such a beautiful, blazing metaphor for the process of transition. In watching the dance between wildfires and wild nature, we see that the end result is life returning with new vigor, abundance, and variety. We see, too, the profundity of the ending that preceded the regrowth and of the black time in between of no new growth at all.

Self, others, place, and *work* have been the foundational pillars of my spirit, which are continually being tested, torn down, rebuilt, and tested again with every ending and every new beginning in my life. "Nothing functions by itself," writes Dr. Carl Hammerschlag. "Family, community, country. Job, education, heritage, home. History, culture, religious beliefs, principles. How we put all these together in our lives makes up the unique individuals we are."[1] I could remember no transition or crisis in my life that had not been—at its core—a call to reconsider and reconstruct my relationship with these interwoven ancestral towers of my soul. These pillars, not coincidentally, also offer us all the tools we need to make a successful transition of any kind.

Self embraces for me my relationship not only with my mental and emotional self but also with the God-self, the part of me that lives in the realms of spirit and mystery. At its root a transition is an urgent homecoming call to self.

Outside of myself are the *others* with whom I am called into relationship—my family, my community, my intimate partner. Although I value my human community deeply, when I am called by life to change and grow, I have found over and over again that the greatest source of help, guidance, wisdom, and spiritual healing is nearly always to be found with the rest of my relations: the "others" beyond the human kingdoms. These include not only animals but insects, plants, rocks, wind, and the elements—what the Lakota people wisely call *Mitaku Oyasin,* or "all my relations." The most sustaining and creative cache of soul medicine awaiting us in times of deep personal change is buried in the hearts and lives of these precious others.

Since we are the youngest children of Creation, our accumulated wisdom is young, too, and so I search outside of the tiny and fragile box of humankind's insight and understanding for the older wisdom, the more ancient and enduring healing. In my previous books, I have documented the rich insights and mercies brought to my life by my animal kin. Because of this, I tell people that I write about animals, which in a way I suppose I do. But in truth I write about the empowerment of meaningful and healing relationships. Many of mine are with animals and nature.

No transition in my life has excluded a review and reevaluation of *work*. Oftentimes, the fires in my world have necessitated a career shift or a redefinition of what I call work. It is my belief that men and women are not whole without meaningful work—that is, work as a force that reveals to us more of our genuine selves and that grounds us to life. No living being is exempted from the joys and the challenges of seeking and manifesting "right livelihood," whether that livelihood be defined as a meaningful career for a human being, a successful swim upstream for a determined salmon, a full nest of eggs hatched and fledged for a robin and her spouse, or the simple work of living through twenty-four hours for one of our many insect kin, who are God-granted only a day or two of life span to achieve their unique dreams. All of us, from the largest to the smallest, are drawn by some ineffable spirit to the sweet call of our life's work. It is the spirit of this work that calls to us in times of change, imploring us to come home to the true manifestation of ourselves in this lifetime.

No fire strikes us in a vacuum. It finds us in our *place*, and the quality, timing, and lessons of a life change are, in a great sense, molded and moved by that place. Place is so much broader and bigger than the boards and roofing shingles above our heads. It is the geography in which we find ourselves. Mountains, cities, shores, deserts—no geography, no place, really claims us by chance. We collude with it, accept it, conjure it, curse it. In my life I have consciously and with great care chosen the geography around me. I have selected it for its energy and for its beauty, often forgoing career opportunities and choices of decent housing just to center myself in certain sustaining landscapes.

The entire living miracle of the Earth is contained in the realms of place, too. She is our largest, first, and most enduring home. Wherever we track upon her face, we are still with her, her energy singing to us the same melody of life and nurture from ocean beaches, city slums, or green woodlands. Following the track of my house fire, I have learned just how deeply place influences us in our transitional journey, coloring our path with its own particular palette of topography, biology, and local culture and likewise offering the same to us as useful gifts in our change process.

Underbedding place, like an aquifer lying dark and still beneath a flowering prairie, lies the enduring notion of home. To be "at home" is to feel a sense of belonging, of being welcomed, wanted, and safe. During times of change and transition, we are stricken with an acute sense of being lost, of wandering homeless and dazed in nearly every important aspect of our lives. When life sends a personal earthquake shuddering beneath my feet, I lose my sense of belonging—of being "at home" with my work, with my friends, and in my house. The feeling of disengagement extends its wet fingers beneath the very bedrock of my life, and I find myself for a time not even feeling at home in my own body. In transition we are offered unique opportunities to come home to a greater sense of belonging in our lives, in our work, in our relationships, and to the Earth herself. Homecoming is the goal of any transition—to come home to a new and hopefully fuller sense of belonging to the world and to our lives. Home is larger than we think. It is harder to create, to destroy, or to leave than we might imagine. And the journey to a soul-felt sense of home is ultimately more crucial to the health of our bodies and souls than we could possibly dream.

My home rests near Jackson Hole, Wyoming, and the Teton Range, and my neighbors are deer, elk, moose, bears, ancient rock and stone, quaking aspens and cottonwoods, and sagebrush and wild rivers. Their teachings, I sensed, would be both startlingly similar to and at the same time vastly different from the lessons offered by the mostly domestic animals and landscapes that had been my teachers for so long. I no longer live among tame and ordered life. My heart lives on the borderlands of the wild. It is my place, and my lessons come to me in the colors and textures of an untamed—and unknown—palette.

Once again animals have led my soul journey and tamped down a path through wild and charred terrain. Especially here in the mountains, the voices and hearts of the animals fill the lands. Certainly the greater Yellowstone ecosystem is in no way immune to human meddling, yet it remains a place where the animal energies are the stronger ones. You cannot live here and *not* feel the presence of Grizzly, Wolf, Deer, and Buffalo as strongly as you would feel the press of human flesh in a city mall. It is not that there are so many animals left here. It is just that their soul in this place is so very, very strong.

The tools I was given to craft and rebuild my spirit

pillars of self, others, work, and place are the foundational chapters of this book: gifts of the value of mystery, magic, and dream weaving; reflections on ritual, generosity and gratitude, and a deeper look into the worth and meaning of community; lessons on the profound value of reframing life's challenges into a picture of unique, personal meaning; animal teachings on intimate partings and unions and on the deep truth of our need for belonging and homecoming. These tools and gifts saw me through fire, despair, and on to a new beginning. My practice of these gifts is just that— practice. It is not necessary to be a master of any or all of them in order to reap their value in times of change.

Rebuild, reconstruct, renew. Immediately these are the places I go in my heart when I have had a burn-down. In the effort to put change behind me as quickly as possible, I hurry along toward the quickest new beginnings I can lay my hands on. My good friend, animal communicator and mystic Sharon Callahan, offers yet another perspective on life transition after fire: "The lowest level of spiritual response to a symbolic fire would be to reconstruct exactly what has been destroyed. The second level would be to construct something just a bit different. The highest spiritual level of transformation would be to not reconstruct at all. The spiritual perspective would be 'to die before you die,' or to dismantle the ego purposefully before death takes it. Can we rise out of constructs altogether?"

I listened to Sharon. Too often I have hurried into a new life that was ill considered because I did not want to face the fallow zone, the seemingly dead zone of a protracted sense of "now what?" This time I resolved to give the transitional process its full due, and there was much in my life that I chose not to rebuild after the blaze. Cradled in the love and wisdom of friends like Sharon, I have been able, in some instances, simply to hold up my empty hands to life and just be still.

In the course of my fire journey, I have struggled to hold one belief foremost in my mind, and it has made the road rockier, more surprising, and of far greater consequence. I choose to believe that every event in my life is of great personal significance, a divine teaching. Gary Zukav writes in *The Seat of the Soul,* "Every experience that you have and will have upon the Earth encourages the alignment of your personality with your soul. Every circumstance and situation gives you the opportunity to choose this path, to allow your soul to shine through you, to bring into the physical world through you its unending and unfathomable reverence for and love of Life."[2]

I would add that every experience we have is the birthing ground of a new life story, and I am a firm believer in the power of story to teach and to heal. Our story, I believe, is the only gift of real value we have to offer another. Everything else in our life is fact, figure, or hearsay. And while we are happy to give these "gifts" often and generously to others, they are of no real consequence. Our stories alone are our truth, a truth that is as solid and enduring as stone. Mixed with the elixir of a well-told story, truth imparted in this way has the power to transform lives and to inspire those it touches.

When asked by an interviewer what really defined an adult, poet and storyteller Robert Bly answered that an adult is someone who can take the disconnected bits and fragments of life and weave them into a story of meaning. This reminds me of cancer surgeon Bernie Siegel's admonition to stop waiting for the meaning in life to come along and knock you in the head, because the only meaning you will find in life is the heartfelt meaning you give it.

Stories are like roses, the petals of their meaning unfolding and falling away so that new meaning is constantly revealed. Often I will look at a story in my life from many different viewpoints over time and be dazzled at the new applications to my life an old story can impart in the retelling. And so this story of fire—of endings, explorations, and beginnings—is my most cherished gift to you. It is also my attempt to assemble the challenging fragments of the past four years of my life into my own story of meaning. I earnestly hope it will encourage you to do the same with the unique and awesome bits and pieces of your own life.

This is a book about fire—the fire that burns up our inner and outermost houses and from which we craft a new life and a new path. It is a book about standing up in the middle of the ash pile, dusting off, and following the ancient, ancestral animal trails—the four-footed path—to our most cherished heart of home.

Susan Chernak McElroy
Jackson Hole, Wyoming

Heart in the Wild

1

Firewalk

*As we wake or sleep
we grow strong or we grow weak.
At last, some crisis shows us
what we have become.*

—Bishop Westcott

The raven circled the column of smoke, which went straight up, blossoming like a fat, black balloon in that windless January afternoon. I thought the bird was soaring over someone's trash pile. *Somebody's really got a heap going*, I told myself. *And right above our house.* Burn piles are commonplace in the rural Wyoming valley where I live. The dark, billowing clouds that always attend them celebrate the site of someone's old haystack, garden clippings, or collapsed outbuilding. And yet something about this burn pile struck me as different. Something about the location. *Where is it coming from? It must be the neighbors just up the road. No, that's not quite right.*

It was four days after the turn of the millennium, and I was returning home all warm and cozy after tea with a friend. The sun was dropping off the horizon, and the late afternoon shadows were dark charcoal. Aspens rested in the foothills, standing bare and serene, with trunks the color of campfire ashes. For me winter in Wyoming is a magic time. There is the cold, yes, but the mountains are so white that they shine even on days when the sun does not. And against that white, the blue of the sky is the color of oceans.

That particular day in early January, the winter landscape had me so captivated that I hadn't noticed the black smoke balloon rising under the crest of our hill until I was approaching the final turn up the road to our house. For several moments I watched the raven playing tag with the smoke, wondering where the gray cloud originated. I felt irritated, imagining that it would waft its way up to our house, sending me into coughing fits when I went up to the barn to feed my horse and donkeys.

The raven abruptly wheeled and spun away to the east. Instantly my body clamped down upon itself. And with a furious and icy rush of dread, I knew. But for a few moments longer—for as long as my mind would allow me to believe that my life had not changed forever—I chose not to know. I do not remember driving the car. I do not remember putting my foot on the brake to slow for the coming turn. I do not remember anything until I spun my wheel to make the turn and saw my corner neighbor, Archie, old and bent like a stick of driftwood, come hurrying to my car, shaking his head from side to side. I looked at Archie's face and then past his face to the columns of red flame moving like a breaking wave across the roof of my house. The raven was a tiny speck on the horizon. Opening the car window, I tasted the bitter chalkiness of smoke against the back of my mouth. Archie leaned in, his face close to mine, his head still shaking from side to side. Now his voice shook, too, and he said, "My God, Susie, I'm sorry. It looks like she's all gone . . . all gone . . ."

In the nightmare of a living dream, I closed the window to block out the smell of smoke and opened my eyes wide, wide, letting the sight take hold, letting my throat clench. My home all in flames. Crowds lining the road. Cars milling everywhere. With my windows closed, it seemed as though all the chaos that I saw was unfolding in utter and eerie silence. The only sound that reached me was a curious muffled thudding, which I finally identified as the sound of my heart pounding like a fist against the walls of my chest.

In those first moments of terrible realization, I struggled to pull air into my compressed lungs in deep, sucking gulps. I could not get enough. My head felt as light and unsubstantial as soapsuds. In my head was a cry, running over and over like a circular tape: *This is NOT happening. This is a dream. This is NOT real. Wake up . . . wake up . . . wake up . . .*

You might think I would have stepped on the gas and careened up the road as fast as the winter ice would let me. I did not. I drove slowly, slowly. It was not only my eyes that were open like a ship's portholes. It was my mouth, too, like a gaping maw, stretching to let out a groan that seemed to come from the very base of my spine. My hands splayed wide for an instant, before clutching the steering wheel only to open wide again. I felt as though I were trying, trying with each piece of my body, to open wide enough to take in the immensity of the horror.

Mom, Mom, Mom. She lived in an apartment downstairs. *Dear God, my mom! The dogs, the cats!*

I pulled into the driveway, the car jerking along the ice-rutted drive, my feet numb on the pedals, my knees locked. In the shadow of the firestorm stood my husband, Lee, with his arm around my mother. Sitting beside my mother were our two dogs, Arrow and Strongheart. As soon as Arrow saw me, she ran up happily beside the car to welcome me home, her glorious brown collie fur dancing in the ghostly light of the flames. So long as her mother—me—was there, she was delighted. *She thinks this is a bonfire*, I thought. *A party* . . . From the car I saw Strongheart, my huge white Anatolian shepherd dog, lean his head protectively against my mother—a position he would not abandon for the coming six hours. A Turkish livestock-guarding dog, he was putting his heritage to work caring for the most fragile in our human herd of three. At a sit his head reached to the middle of my mom's chest. Unlike Arrow, he seemed deeply affected by the flames and the noise of the fire. His wide brow was furrowed, and his kind, bold face registered a mix of distress and concern.

I realized that I needed to make space for the fire trucks, which didn't seem to be there yet. In a daze, still gasping for the air that would not come, I pulled forward, then reversed, then turned around in a circle. My head was beginning to pound. Where to go? Where *was* there to go? I parked the car on the street and walked on stiff legs to my family. My head was shaking from side to side in stunned disbelief. My family's eyes were wide, like my own. Their mouths were tight. "What happened?" I gasped. They shook their heads. We didn't know. Days later we would learn that an extension cord had shorted out and sparked the fire. We used that cord to plug in the block heater of our plow truck, and the plug and cord were located just to the left of a neck-high stack of firewood stored on the porch by our garage. The firewood had provided ample fuel to torch the rest of the house.

Mom rubbed her hands together. She was standing in the snow in a thin pair of knitted slippers and seemed completely oblivious to the freezing cold. She had escaped with Arrow and Strongheart and with Flora and Dinky—two of our four cats. I could hear a thin edge of guilt creeping into her voice. Two cats still remained in the house: Red, Mom's beach ball–sized orange cat, and Mirella, my beloved, dainty, silver tabby. Red was old, almost thirteen, and Mirella just a baby at four.

I ran up to the volunteer firemen, who were waiting helplessly for the fire trucks to arrive, and in blubbering tears begged them to let me enter the house to search for my cats. They stood protectively near the front door in full gear with tanks strapped to their backs and would not let me pass. Lamely I told them I would hold my breath. They shook their heads and motioned me back. After what seemed like days, the fire trucks pulled into the driveway. The firemen grabbed hoses as thick as boa constrictors and plunged into the house.

I shouted after them to search in my office, hoping the cats would be there, praying that they would be there: my office was the room farthest away from the flames and smoke. Red loved to sit on the office couch while I worked, licking his feet and purring like a jet engine. Mirella frequently napped on my desk or swatted at the rocks and figurines atop my office altar table. If they were in my office, perhaps I would see them alive again.

As the firemen disappeared into waving curtains of smoke, I felt a familiar hand rest lightly on my shoulder.

Turning, I looked into the weathered face of David, my Cherokee friend and spiritual teacher. Somehow, in this small and tight-knit community, word had reached him about the fire, and he had come from his cabin on the mountain to stand vigil with me. His silver hair shone in the firelight. Around his neck the signature bear claw shimmered back the reflection of the flames. He told me softly that everything would be OK.

When life strikes me broadside, I field the blow by diving swiftly and completely into action. I'm not saying that I am effective in my action—only that I stay busy. Facing the fire, I wanted nothing more than to keep busy and, most of all, to keep from thinking. I ran everywhere, talking to all the firefighters, telling them where the roof accesses were, telling them again where I thought the cats might be. Lee stayed at the other side of the house, giving directions from there. Parts of the house were beginning to collapse in his direction, and for a moment I feared they would fall on him as he struggled to move some of our outside belongings away from the path of the fire.

The firemen reached my office and from an open window shouted to me that they could see nothing beneath the furniture. I couldn't tell if they meant that there was nothing there or that the smoke was too thick to see anything. While they were still in the office, I told them to throw my computer, research books, and file cabinets out the windows and onto the snow. Piling the stuff onto blankets donated by our neighbors, I hauled the heap that represented all of my working life away from the blazing house and onto the driveway.

Around the side of the house, I discovered Flora and Dinky, our other two cats, huddled fearfully together at the

bottom steps to my mom's apartment, trying to get back inside. "Not a good idea. . . ," I said, grabbing them and stuff-
ing them inside my jacket. Flora had survived leukemia as a
kitten. This night she had beaten death once again. Dinky
had been completely blind since birth, and I whispered a
prayer of thanksgiving that he hadn't run off somewhere in
sightless terror. He was a coal-black cat who could, under
the circumstances, easily have been mistaken for a glob of
soot, and I couldn't imagine trying to find him in the dark.
For lack of a better place to confine them, I put both cats
into the chicken shed across the driveway. As I shut the
door behind me, I heard the surprised clucking of my four
laying hens. Dinky was certainly no threat to them, and
Flora had hunted nothing larger than a bug in thirteen years,
so I figured the chickens would be fine and left it at that for
the time being.

Behind all my frenzied action, I heard the language of
that fire. It spoke to me with a joyous roar, a cry that for all
its destructive power sounded full and free and deeply satis-
fied. Its voice embraced the high-pitched shattering of windows; the low, explosive thunder of collapsing beams; the
giddy sputtering of white-hot wood. When the flames
reached the boxes of ammunition in the garage, there was
the *rat-tat-tat* of bullets singing like firecrackers.

I remember stopping, spellbound, to watch the flames
gorge upon the garage and kitchen until the roof collapsed
with a thud, sending a horde of sparks into the winter sky. I
remember thick clouds of greasy, acrid-smelling smoke billowing out the broken doors and windows like a mass of
raging buffalo. I remember how the fire ate and ate and
would not stop. I remember the nausea rising in my throat.

And I remember, too, a knowing nearly impossible to

describe, that this fire would come, and had come. A quiet, deep part of me—furtive and lithe and strong as a hunting weasel—felt no surprise at the sight of the flames. I had seen or felt this fire—as though I had conversed with it before I ever came to Earth. At a very visceral level, I knew that I had agreed that this fire should take my house and that we would dance together in this way.

Around me neighbors huddled. One sobbed in deep, moaning wails. Dozens of us raced around the slippery grounds like displaced ants, bumping into one another in our frantic attempts to convince ourselves that our scurrying about could accomplish something. Two hours passed.

I was kneeling on the ground, spent and tear-streaked, when a fireman approached me with two limp bundles of fur in his gloved hands. I opened my arms and pulled Red and Mirella close against my chest. Their small, loose bodies felt boneless, but miraculously they were still alive. Their yellow eyes gazed at me sightlessly from faces caked with wet soot. I carried them to the waiting ambulance, and a kind emergency technician laid them both on the front seat of the ambulance and gently placed oxygen masks on their small faces. Mirella resisted, swatting at the mask and batting the hands of the ambulance driver. "It's a good sign," he smiled. "She's feeling good enough to be cranky." Red lay still, not moving, not complaining. I turned back to the fire, shaking with grief and exhaustion. I could not know then that the cats would recover, though it would take many days, or that Red would lose his voice permanently to smoke damage. It seemed impossible to me in those dark moments that lasted for hours that anything could have come out of that house alive.

After leaving Red and Mirella to the care of the emergency workers, I went back toward the house. The flames were withering, finally, and the sounds of gushing hoses and dripping water were replacing the deafening roar of the retreating fire. My bones and muscles ached, and I was suddenly overtaken by a weariness beyond words. I could not for one moment longer keep running, keep doing. Legs shaking, I sank down in the snow near a comforting spruce tree. I searched for more tears, simply because they seemed an appropriate response to the situation, but they would not come. The stillness of my body made room for the events of the evening to begin seeping into my consciousness, and I fought it. *I'll fall apart if I feel this*, I told myself. *I'm too tired to feel any of this yet. I won't feel this . . .*

My eyes squeezed shut to block out the sight of my home standing in the dark, burned, crushed, and smoking. When I opened them again, I saw in the shadow of the ruins everything that meant anything to me in my life: my work, piled in a jumbled heap in the snow; husband, family, friends, and neighbors—my human community—talking in hushed, almost reverent tones; my animal family—cats and dogs—milling confused in the driveway; my horse skull—totem symbol of my spiritual life and protector of my home—gazing with black eye sockets from the broken porch; my lovely mountain home itself, all in tatters. All of these beings and all of these things had been touched in some deep and as yet inexplicable way by the sooty fingers of the fire. Each had died in some way from the crushing events of the evening. Life as I had come to know it was over.

A quiet thought bubbled up: *It is good that this life is over. It was too big*. For an instant I saw myself standing in the door of a tiny house, living a simpler life. Looking at the foundation of my home, which was still intact, I buried the thought of smaller and simpler—comforting as it felt in those moments—in the back recesses of my brain. The house would need to be reconstructed on its frame. And the five acres around it had not shrunk. The work of maintaining such a large place was daunting enough when life was running smoothly. I shuddered to think of my workload now.

I stood up and rubbed my wet, near-frozen behind and walked up the path to the barn to feed my horse and donkeys. Somehow I had completely forgotten my barn family in the events of the evening. As I walked along the snowy fence line three sweet-smelling equine muzzles greeted me, blowing hay-perfumed steam against my cheek. Fashion, my horse, and Polani and Aurora, the miniature donkeys, were delighted as usual to see me. None seemed the least bit disturbed by the fire, the smoke, or the endless commotion on the driveway below them. In low, quiet tones I explained to "the girls" what was happening and felt the power of words spoken out loud work their magic to settle the unsteadiness of my heart. They watched me intently all the time I was speaking. When my words ran out, they put their noses down into the hay that I parceled out to them and began the soft, rhythmic chewing that always calmed my wild mind and settled my spirit. I stayed with them, patting them in reassurance, but of course, it was they who reassured me. Walking back to the house after my barn time, I felt the first small measure of peace I had found all evening.

It had all begun at about four in the afternoon. It wasn't until after ten that night that the firemen, grimy with soot and the sweat of exhaustion, began packing up to leave. One said wryly as he turned to go, "Don't worry. It will look worse in the morning." At that point my home was a smoking mass of charred lumber and blackened wires. One half was completely gone. We could not see into the smoky remains to know what—if anything—had been spared. We had been told repeatedly by the fire crew to expect the worst—to expect a total loss. After most of the crew had left, and the trucks and neighbors mostly departed, Terry, the fire chief, approached me and put her hand softly on my arm. "Would you like to take a look inside?" she asked. I nodded and went to find Lee.

Terry passed out flashlights, and we all stepped up through the half-inch-thick layer of ash in the driveway to the front doorjamb. The crew had placed enormous fans in front of the doors, and the bulk of the smoke had been blown away. We snapped on our flashlights in unison and aimed them inside. The remaining wisps of smoke filtered our light, but we could make out the sofa and chairs in the living room. Terry led us slowly inside, flipping her flashlight beam through the room. Suddenly she stopped and sucked in a deep breath. "I . . . I don't believe this," she murmured. "I just . . . don't . . . believe it . . ."

The yellow beams from our flashlights bounced crazily across sooted walls and groupings of neatly placed furniture all covered with gray ash the color of old, old dust. Water dripped everywhere, splattering down from the edges of the lampshades and table knickknacks. The large living room windows were opaque with smoke. The dark green carpet was awash in inches of blackened water, like a shallow, lifeless lake. But *it was intact!* The kitchen, dining room, and garage were gone, but everything else remained. Terry turned to us with a look of absolute astonishment on her face. "I just can't believe this. I expected this to be a burned-out shell. The way the fire moved . . . the flames . . . how in the *world* could this have been spared?"

The roof was gone, yet the entire ceiling remained whole. But for the sour smell of wet smoke, you could almost imagine that the back half of the house was simply inhabited by a family of total slobs and that nothing like a fire had ever touched it. "You would be amazed at what can be done these days to clean up smoke damage," Terry told us, flashing her light up the streaked walls. "This place will be like new again. Just like new. You'll see." She hugged Lee and me as we stood in stunned silence. Behind her relief and delight lurked an unsettling knowing in me that "good as new" would not apply here. The fire had signaled an abrupt end—of what, I could not yet know.

Lee and I had both seen enough this night, bad and good. It was time for us to leave, to breathe, to be alone and silent, and to begin absorbing the past six hours. Neighbors took us into their homes that night. Mom and the dogs and cats went to stay with the Romeos, who lived behind us, and Lee and I were invited in by the Balsars, who lived just above us. We crawled into a warm and unfamiliar bed that night and hung on to each other, tight and wordless in the dark.

Sleep never came for me the night of the fire. Lee dozed fitfully. Too tired to cry, too shocked to sleep, I slipped into a state of semiconsciousness, the place where the mists that separate this world from the realms of spirit are most thin. In this hazy, sparkling between-world, I imagined my arms around the neck of an enormous and peaceful bull elk. He was mature and strong, as big as a horse, with antlers tall and branched like old, hard trees. I could feel the bristles of his winter coat warm and rough against my cheek. He smelled of smoke. We stood in a snow-blanketed pasture, secure and safe in his winter home. My home was no longer a place of safety. For months it would not serve as a haven of any sort. I was suddenly homeless.

The homelessness that had invaded my physical world was new and shocking. But the felt sense of it was naggingly familiar to me. By "felt sense" I mean a deep sense of body knowing, a knowing that steps out of your mind and speaks to you from somewhere else—your stomach, your spine, your heart, your throat. Learning to discover the felt sense that lurked beneath my intellectual understanding of things was something I'd worked hard to achieve, and I listened closely anytime my body spoke to me in this visceral, important way. My mind has been known to trick me, but my body always speaks the truth.

I whispered confidingly to the elk that the sense of not really ever belonging anywhere was a dark and mean-spirited creature that had camped on the very periphery of my interior landscape for as long as I could remember. Homelessness had been with me in my cancer years, a time of cataclysmic inner and outer transition as my body tried seriously to evict me—homelessness in its most graphic manifestation. The sense of not belonging anywhere, of having my life turned inside out, was strong in me then. I thought I had overcome that. Now it had returned.

Coming home is a process without end. Like the turning of seasons, the heart of belonging rolls around again, like tides, like high mountain lakes thawing and freezing and thawing again. Another chance to look at homecoming—feeling safe, valued, and welcomed in life, work, and community— is the greatest promise of transitional times and the gift most overlooked. Tears welled up in my eyes, and I buried them in the coarse fur of Elk's thick, powerful neck. Why was I being challenged again so harshly? *Why me?* My voice against his neck sounded fragile and small and pockmarked with guilt.

Why not? was his candid reply.

The elk settled down with a grunt in deep, dry snow, and I sank down beside him, resting my cheek on his flank. I stroked the thick, hollow winter hairs over his muscled shoulder and asked him to tell me about fire. The elk snorted out dense puffs of white steam into the black night air, and I understood his silent words. I understood that fire finds us all—some in the burning of relationships, some in the flame of disease, some in the inferno of dreams never lived and never dared. Fire burns us each day, uniquely and with smoldering effectiveness. Placing my hands over the heart of this elk, I asked him why fire had come for me, and to me.

He looked at me with liquid brown eyes and sniffed gently along the cancer scar line etched on my jaw, running down to my collarbone. In his eyes I could see the reflection of yellow flames. This elk had known fire, and known it well.

This fire was a harbinger of change, he told me, an outer expression of an inner burning that would become clear in the coming year. It was a transition made so clear that it could be touched like charred boards held in your hands—a transition that could be seen with the eyes so that one would understand without question that the transformation from wood to ash to life again was real and true. Like cancer, it was a gift—a lifelong, rich gift. Not poison, but good.

With the smell of smoke in my throat and the barest inkling of the journey before me, I pressed my face to the pillow and whispered a small thank-you to the elk. And as the first gray light of dawn rose on the eastern horizon, I cautiously thanked the fire.

2

Exile

Most people are on the world, not in it—
have no conscious sympathy or relationship to anything about them—
undiffused, separate, and rigidly alone like marbles of polished stone,
touching but separate.
—John Muir

Morning coffee tasted comforting and pungent, and I gripped the hot mug until my knuckles went white. *Insurance,* I thought. *Call the insurance company. Call them. Call your brother. Call friends. What's left? It'll take a million boxes to empty out what's left of the house. Oh, NO, not another move . . . Not another one. Where will we stay? Rent a motel room? House? Are the cats still alive this morning?*

I had stayed in bed late the morning after the fire, not to sleep but to avoid what I knew would be an assault to my senses when I returned to my house. From our neighbors' cozy living room, I could look down the road to the northern end of our place. It had snowed long and hard during the night, and my home looked remarkably serene. Only the gaping roof gave away the events of the night before.

The roar of thoughts in my head continued as Lee and I drove down the road to the house. Snow had covered everything, like the crisp, white sheet the morticians had brought to my mother's house to cover the body of my father. *Yes, I* thought. *White to cover the dead. White to commemorate endings and beginnings. Snow white to cover my home that died last night.* In the aspen trees outside the house, flocks of winter birds were singing brilliantly. Chickadees, pine siskins, and Cassin's finches flooded the empty bird feeders and picked at small dots of ash on the snow. I dragged a bag of sunflower seeds out of a snow pile and fed the birds, grateful for the brightness of their songs.

We walked first through the hopeful end of the house. In the mostly empty space of my office, whose contents were now bundled in blankets in the back of our car, I found a water-stained picture of Jackson Lake and the Tetons. It had been sent to me by a reader of my books and had been an office fixture of mine long before I had moved back to this part of the country. "Hope you like the pictures. Jackson Lake is a favorite place of mine. —Fritz Saam." It was a favorite of mine, too. I crumpled up the soggy photo and dropped it to the floor with the rest of the wet papers that had not made it out the window the previous night.

Lee headed outside to check out the carnage around the garage, and I slipped wordlessly into the battered remains of the kitchen. The fireman was indeed correct: my home looked much worse in the daylight. Its scorched, wire-veined flesh hung painfully exposed in the weak rays of morning sun. Everywhere the blistered skin of board and Sheetrock

was peeled and hanging and ruined. I had never realized
how much insulation is in a house. It was everywhere, piled
more than two feet deep on the countertops and in the
sinks. Underfoot it mounded up into a small landscape of
frozen hills and valleys, grabbing my feet with every step
and threatening to pull me down hard. Through the open
ceiling, snow continued its slow, mournful fall.

The fire had struck on January 5, Strongheart's third
birthday. It was the very day I had begun to write this book.
I was forty-eight years old, a time, astrologically, when you
are said to be wrapping up your old life to begin a completely new cycle. That morning I didn't feel new in any way.
I felt old and shriveled, and I had seen all my tired eyes could
bear for one morning. Pulling up the hood on my coat, I hurried back to my room at the neighbors' and crawled swiftly
into bed, hauling the covers up over my face.

In the back of my skull, just between the place where
the head ends and the neck begins, Elk snorted against my
skin and whispered to me about home. Wasn't it true, he
asked, that my postfire feelings were new in degree but certainly not in kind? I took a long breath and asked myself
when I could remember a similar tone of feeling, something that felt like the fire loss but maybe not quite so extreme. My body spoke quickly, recalling such feelings in
the company of my family, friends, and workmates and
in the process of work itself. I remembered muffled pangs of
not being "at home" in my intimate relationships and with
my own body.

Yet stretching its long arms over the myriad arenas
of homelessness that had called to me in insistent, high-
pitched voices was an immense loneliness that blanketed all

the others: I was acutely aware of a strong, stabbing sense of not feeling at home in Wyoming or, for that matter, on Earth.

The thought shook me: not even at home on Earth. Since my return to the Rocky Mountains three years before, I had felt a bone-deep loss, a sense that the Earth was not welcoming me as a wild daughter. Outside of suburbia I had no true place, no heart's home. The other feelings of not belonging in my life paled before this greater loneliness, as though work, relationships, and spiritual belonging were simply rooms whose doors were closed to me. My loss of a sense of home on Earth, however, was like losing the whole house—which is exactly, I realized, what had happened to me.

Intuitively and immediately I knew that if I could find ways of healing this deep wounding—this sense of not belonging to the very Earth—I could begin to construct new and enduring heart-based rooms in all the other areas in my life in which I had for years felt so orphaned. I could rest at home, then, in body, heart, and soul. The sudden, unbidden change in my life precipitated by the fire offered me an opportunity to more fully realize homecoming—a challenge that I realized I had not yet mastered in my cancer transition thirteen years before, or in my move back to the Rocky Mountains. Each of those changes in my life had helped me to mature and had gifted me with bright-colored snippets of the fabric of homecoming, but not yet enough of the cloth to pull comfortably around my shoulders.

Moving to Wyoming had been no small undertaking. I had given up Brightstar Farm, my cherished Oregon home, to follow the path that led me back to the Tetons. Brightstar Farm had been the first home I had ever owned, an enchanting place of one lush green acre blanketed in trees, grass, and flowers. In the brief five years I lived there, the ground had become a part of my being. I loved the place, the barn, the animals, the neighbors. Brightstar was, in the strongest sense, "me." Only the power of my lifelong love for the Tetons could have called me away from that small plot of precious ground, and even that call was not enough to fill the hole in my heart that Brightstar left behind: I had seen only the dream of the Tetons and of my new life in Wyoming. I never stopped to mourn what I was leaving behind. It was a loss that was to haunt me for years.

But my call to the Rockies was a genuine call of the soul. The land had beckoned to me in a voice of absolute conviction when I was only six years old. This did not happen in the normal way, which would have been a family vacation. Jackson Hole and the Tetons had called me through my television set. One summer evening when the crickets were in full song outside our California bungalow, I'd watched, mesmerized, as the Teton mountain range danced across the screen in a Disney show titled "One Day at Teton Marsh." Destiny had spoken to me like the voice of God, booming from the voice box of a black-and-white Zenith TV. I turned to my mother and said, "When I graduate from high school, I'm going to work at Teton Marsh."

"You do that, dear," she replied. I don't suppose she ever gave the comment a second thought. I forgot about it completely myself until my senior year in high school. But three weeks before high school graduation, I packed a square blue suitcase with jeans and hiking boots and took all my finals early. Bypassing my senior prom, senior cut day, and graduation ceremonies, I headed off to the Rockies to do what God had told me to do when I was six.

I lived in Jackson Hole for seven years in my late teens and early twenties, and the valley had hooked teeth in me that went deep. Eventually economics forced me to leave. Town closed down as tightly as an agitated box turtle in the winter, and jobs were as scarce as fairy dust. I went back to California, but so intense was my longing to return that my love for the Tetons became a constant theme in my sleeping and waking dreams and in my writing. Every vacation brought me back to the Tetons, over and over again. I would laugh about returning regularly to my Jackson "shrine" to worship at the foot of the Tetons, but it was really no joke. That is exactly what I was doing.

When the initial royalties from *Animals as Teachers and Healers* rolled in, offering me the first financial breathing space I had ever had, my Teton dream rekindled and began burning fiercely. Within a year Lee and I had packed up farm and family and moved to a new home on the outskirts of Jackson Hole.

When I had long ago lived in Jackson Hole in my late teens, I dreamed, as very young people can dream, that the land and the beauty all around me were some sort of lovely aesthetic effect made just for my enjoyment, much like background music in a movie. I did not view the magnificent animals all around me—swans, buffalo, elk, moose, badgers, eagles—as sacred beings on sacred ground with destinies of their own.

In truth, my childhood love for animals and nature had often been a greedy sort of love. I took from living Creation all that my heart wanted, to the virtual exclusion of the needs of those living beings whose life I invaded out of my own selfish need for some sort of connection with a world that was secret and captivating to me. The allure of wild things was powerful and deeply compelling. So much in contrast with the domesticity, regimentation, and predictability of life in my small California factory town, wildlife and wild places represented qualities absent in my life, like freedom, surprise, and awe.

My child mind translated this undefinable attraction into simple body terms. In short, my desire to know wildness went straight to my small hands. I wanted to touch the wild and to absorb its gifts and mysteries through my skin. Pet shops back then sold all manner of wild beings, and at one time or another, I possessed nearly all of them. For years a fat golden-mantled ground squirrel lived in a hamster cage on our kitchen counter. A kangaroo rat came to stay for a while. I would have bought a raccoon kit or even an ocelot baby, but I didn't have enough money, so I settled for a box turtle and a baby boa constrictor the size of a pencil.

I captured snakes and kept them in tanks on the back porch. One summer my brother and I caught hundreds of tiny toads to feed our reptile family. We crammed them tightly in a small aquarium that held them three layers deep. Of course, we were too busy with our summer play to find enough food for them or even to keep their water bowl full, and most of them died of starvation or dehydration. I would pull their skinny, lifeless bodies out of the tank each day and ignore the black stabs of remorse.

I raised many orphaned baby birds, delighting in the feel of their hollow-boned fragility against my cheek. There was just something about the sensation of holding wildness in my hands that overruled any natural hesitation I might have had about how deeply I was disturbing the lives and fates of those wild beings.

In my first decades of life, I was a too-ready and obedient student of my cosmology—our origin story—which reminded me daily in every form of media that the Earth and all of her Creation were mine. And so animals remained mine to buy or capture, study and grasp, mine to keep. They were God's legacy to me: the culture held me blameless in my need to pet, caress, hold, and imprison those who were helpless to evade me.

With the exception of the toads, I believed that I gave my captives the best of care. That they were captives was only in the infancy stages of being an ethical concern of mine. "The world belongs to man" is the deadly proclamation of our culture and our religious institutions, warns author Daniel Quinn in his series of powerful books about the human story. It was the voice I grew up with.

In the spring of my tenth year, I discovered a large cage of chipmunks for sale at my local pet shop. Instantly I was pointing out the two I wanted to the shop owner. A loner myself, I selected the two chipmunks in the cage of maybe thirty who huddled in a corner away from the rest of the chipmunk crowd. The shop owner netted them, then grabbed them tightly with heavily gloved hands. The entire cageful had been live-trapped in the Lake Tahoe area. None had been hand-raised, and all were terrified. I bought a small book called *Know Your Chipmunk* and set them up in a cage near the ground squirrel on the kitchen counter. In that first week, I saw little of them. They cowered in a nest they made of torn Kleenex and a demolished red bandana, and my attempts at communing with them left me with bite marks on most of my fingers. The following week I returned home from school to a startling announcement from my mother. "Congratulations," she said, greeting me at the door. "Your chipmunk had babies." Suddenly I understood why at least one of them had separated herself from the crowd at the pet shop.

Peering into the cage, I could see that "Mother" had taken over the nest and that her roommate was curled into a tight ball in the corner of the cage, trying to make herself invisible to the monster—me. One tiny pink baby the size of a pinto bean was squirming near the entrance to the den. It must have forgotten to let go of its mother's teat when she left the nest for food or water. I hurried to my chipmunk instruction book and looked for advice: "Should your chipmunk have babies, which is very rare in captivity, they will be abandoned or eaten. Chipmunks will not raise young in captivity." I was not deterred. Since the color picture on the cover of the book was of a golden-mantled ground squirrel—not a chipmunk at all—I told myself that the authors probably didn't know anything about chipmunks anyway.

I reached gently into the cage, trying not to frighten the roommate, and picked up the baby. It was hairless, blind, and soft as a flower petal. I could feel the intense heat of it through my fingers, and the life of it, and the miracle of it, all there in my hand. Carefully I pushed it back into the entrance of the nest and was greeted by Mother, who snatched the baby indignantly out of my fingers and hauled it out of sight.

In the following days, I moved the roommate to a solitary cage of her own and provided nesting materials and

plenty of food. I let her be, which is more than I did for
Mother and her four babies. Every day my hands were inside the nest, extricating a baby to thrill at the excitement
of their growth and development. By their second day of
life, the markings of chipmunkhood were already clearly
upon them, the signature black-and-white stripes running
up past their closed eyes and onto their pinpoint noses.
Within two weeks their eyes had opened, and they were
covered with silky fur.

Mother, for some reason I can only define as mystery, allowed my clumsy intrusions. Strangely she offered me more
than frightened tolerance. I could feel her body calmly shift
aside to make room for my probing fingers. After my inspec-
tion I would leave the babies at the entrance to her elaborate nest, and she would come forward and roll them away
from me, pulling them carefully backward into her cavern,
her eyes on mine.

I offered her corn on the cob, apples, and pine nuts, and
she began to take them gently from my fingers. Even at ten,
I understood that she was a marvel of courage and character,
so diligently caring for her babies in such a foreign and
frightening landscape and so very tolerant of my gross intrusion in her family life.

Although I believed I was absorbed solely in the lives of
the infants, who were beginning to creep from the nest and
explore their—let's be honest here—jail, I found myself reflecting darkly on the lives of the adults as well. Handled
from the day they were born, the fabulous four babies ac-
cepted me fully into their lives and behaved like contented
chipmunks do. They were living bundles of unbridled joy,
animated in their chatter, acrobatic in their play, exuberant
in every aspect of their young lives. The adults—Mother

and the exiled roommate—were, by comparison, not chip-munks at all but some kind of empty, gray-spirited shadow creatures. Although she would accept my probing and my food treats, Mother did not venture out of her nest when her babies did. She spent her days in the dark of her elabo-rate tunnel in mounds of Kleenex and crept from her cave at night, dashing back inside quickly if I turned on the light. The roommate, I never saw at all. Except for the fact that the food disappeared from the bowl and the water from its hanging bottle, the cage might just as well have been empty.

The difference in life vitality between the young chip-munks and the adults was alarming, sobering, and finally painful. For the first time, I was forced to consider that the wild beings in my bondage would choose other lives if they could. When the babies were six weeks old, I snatched Mother away from them with gloved hands and put her into the cage with the invisible roommate. The following morning my family drove to the woods surrounding Lake Tahoe, and I set them free. They never looked back. Why would they?

The babies stayed with me. Two, I gave to friends. The other two lived free in my bedroom, tunneling through the box spring of my bed, leaping up my legs to nuzzle my cheeks when I returned home from school. The babies were my friends. The adults had been my teachers. The chip-munks had provided me with my first taste of myself as jailer, and it was a lesson not soon forgotten. Although I would be years in learning to let wild things just be, the chipmunks had blasted a crack in my human-centered worldview, and the light was beginning to creep in.

By the time I first traveled to the Tetons as a teenager, I had released my captive family of wild animals but had still not awakened to the notion that part of me was a wild animal, too, and that in some perverse way, I was every bit as much a hostage in my culture as were the wildlings I had kept in my house.

Returning to live in Wyoming, I found ghosts of the young woman I had once been watching silently from our old haunts. We had grown apart. Cancer had altered my life path and led me to a deeper and more respectful relationship with animals. I had written two books and contributed to numerous others that spoke to the sacredness and kinship of all life. In my personal credo, I had vowed to write and speak on behalf of animals as beings of great spiritual significance. With so much change between who I had been and who I had become, I was alarmed to find that I no longer felt at home in Wyoming. In my pilgrimage back to the Tetons, with the aching loss of my magical farm lodged in my chest, I had in my own heart become an outcast.

I remembered Oregon as a land of green pastoral reciprocity, where the animals and the countryside had been under a human hand for many generations. The earth that lay beneath my feet there was heavily manhandled, the farm animals docile and compliant. In farm country I was needed: to feed the flocks, to tend the fences, to plant the seeds. It was easy for me to find at least a nurturing familiarity in so heavily domestic and traditional a landscape. Wild beings were allowed in my neighboring community only by invitation. Those not welcome—like coyotes—were dispatched with little fanfare. Skunks were shot, moles trapped, crows cursed. It is the way of things in too much of rural and semirural America.

But Wyoming was a land that bore far less of a human footprint. One winter evening on the wind-scoured plains surrounding my house, hunched against a brutal onslaught of drowning snows and deathly cold, I discovered the night-black forms of massive animals lurking just beyond the range of my flashlight beacon. A herd of migrating elk had bedded down in my driveway like a mass of snow-covered boulders. The temperatures had dropped far below zero, and the snow stung my face as I peered through the darkness at animals all around me. They did not move. Any movement in winter is a critical expenditure of energy, and in the midst of a storm, not a bit of energy is to be wasted. Even a short burst of fearful galloping can mean the difference between life and death for these animals. So they remained in unearthly stillness, aware of me, yet completely disinterested. The elk looked to me for nothing. I was not part of their world in any way. I left them there in the driveway and hurried back to a house that protected me from snow, from wind, and from dark.

At Brightstar Farm the only animals in my yard were stock animals that belonged to me. In such bad weather, I would have hurried them into a straw-bedded barn and closed the door to the snow and wind. A tank of water warmed by an electric water heater would have awaited them, along with deep piles of hay. I was an active, necessary part of the world of the barn. But the winter world of the elk was one I could enter only for brief periods as a stranger, fortified with thermal wear and a cell phone.

Our souls—mine and the elk's—had nothing to say to each other, our common language having been lost aeons ago. Could I be anything to the elk but a bother? My pasture fencing was just one more obstacle to be overcome along their ancestral migration paths, my home a wooden barricade stealing just a few more feet of vital grassland.

How could I belong here, in a place where I was not only not needed but where my life seemed no more than a bungled intrusion into the natural order of things?

I told a neighbor about this absurd idea I had of wanting to build a barn for the elk. She laughed and told me how she had been thinking that maybe she should construct something like a carport for the deer herd in her yard, as though these animals had not done quite fine without us, thank you, for millions of years.

Worse than my feeling of simply not belonging in this wild landscape was my shameful fear of doing damage. "First, do no harm" is a piece of advice aimed at doctors, but the realm of healing is not limited to those with medical degrees. We are all potential healers of the people and places in our lives, bound to our own Hippocratic oath.

Leafing through a magazine on Rocky Mountain living, I came across a full-page drawing of an antlered deer dashing in front of a car. The ad read, "What will you do when animals strike your car this winter?" It was an ad for car insurance. I laughed sarcastically. *Right, the animals run into our cars. Poor cars!* How insane to depict deer in glossy ads as cardenting machines. How starkly in contrast to that ad was the image of deer as "brothers and sisters" in the books I was reading that winter by nature writers, ecologists, and Native Americans. I believed then that the ad was nothing more than a foolish picture—remote, absurd, and out of touch with real life. The terrible reality of deer and cars, however, would strike close to my home less than three weeks later.

Lee and I were driving home late from a movie when I saw a doe lying by the side of the road, gazing out toward the National Elk Refuge—a lovely creature, large and fat from a good summer crop of grass. Our car had already passed her before it struck me that *deer do not bed down on the side of the road.* "Turn around," I told Lee. We swung across an icy highway, turned back, and saw her in the headlights almost instantly. She had been hit hard by a car. Her back end was to the highway, her delicate front feet, like two twisted reeds, pointed toward the refuge. *Refuge.* There would be no refuge for her this night or any night. Pulling her front legs beneath her, she struggled weakly to stand, but her back end remained as motionless as a stone, no doubt broken. In the headlights of our car, her white rump loomed like a luminescent moon fallen to Earth. She swiveled her head side to side on a neck as fine and strong as a lance, eyes seeing everything or nothing.

I stepped out of the car and stood in bright moonlight with snow crystals dancing like fairies in the midnight air all around me. This, I thought, feeling my heart crack open, was the deer in the ad. One of those deer who "strike" cars. My heart cried out to her, *You have been seen. We will take care of you as best we can.* The night was completely still, and I was so close to the doe that I could hear her breathing. I was overcome with the urge to run to her and wrap my arms around her thin neck and sob a blubbering apology. But she let me know with a soft tilt of her head, in the direct and quiet language of animals, just how close I could come without invading and increasing her private agony. And so I stood facing her in the most enormous silence I have ever heard, helpless, angry, and broken inside. *First, do no harm.* The car that struck her on that icy, slick road could just as easily have been mine. Just in the course of living, I was a danger to life.

Again, I was struck with the feeling I could not shrug off: I had no place here in this moment. I did not belong to the deer, to the refuge, to the stars, or to the blue moon-light. I stood a foreigner to this horror, outside of it, unwelcome and uneasy in the time and the place. The moment bloomed tragic and holy all at the same time.

Lee waited while I stood there for long moments, unable to take my eyes from the broken animal in front of me. She was breathtakingly beautiful—still and regal even in the midst of this horror. *So it ends here. No more fawns, no more delicate footprints in new snow, no more autumn nights or springs wet with new grass.* It would all cease for her this night with a bullet to her small head, her final punishment for the tragic mistake of striking someone's car.

We hailed a passerby and used his cell phone to call the sheriff. I was shocked and furious to learn that we were the first people to report the accident. My eyes streaming hot tears, I got into our car. Soon the sheriff would come to shoot her. Her body would become winter food for the ravens and magpies and coyotes who watched the highways in quiet anticipation. As we pulled away, the doe stared with stricken eyes toward the refuge, her broken rump white and motionless as the moon.

Who had hit her, and why did they not stop? Had they been trained by too many ads to see deer as assault weapons, attacking cars with terminal body blows? How could anyone see a living animal as a road bump? What great chasm existed between the writers of the books I was reading and the writers of the gruesome ad that had suddenly lived itself out before my eyes? The answers became brutally clear to me in the coming weeks as the vision of the doe refused to release its hold on me.

In the dark and lonely cultural landscape where we collectively shift our vision of deer from "brother" to insurance event, we become the homeless. We become orphans on Earth, losing touch with our true mother, not because she has abandoned us but because we have run away from her as fast as trains and cars and planes can carry us. But for myself I could not run away from the dying deer. The memory of her kept calling to me, and I knew that some measure of her death had been to bring me a lesson in loneliness that I would not forget.

Two months later my friend Leslie came to visit me. We put on snowshoes one afternoon and walked deep into the woods of Teton Park. Our path crossed over the tracks of many animals. Deep indentations and bits of fur in the snow marked places where elk and moose had rested. Chickadees spoke to us from the trees, and a raven followed after us for a while, calling out with a hollow-sounding *quork-quork-quork*. We stopped to rest in a glade of aspen trees, marveling at the absolute silence. Leslie pulled off her winter hat to hear the quiet better, dusted the snow off her pants, and said in a hushed tone, "I don't feel worthy to be here." Her head was bent, her eyes staring at the snowy ground that sparkled like a jewel in the winter sun.

In seven clipped words, she captured the struggle I had been facing since my return to the valley. But for her *here* meant that particular place of silence and wonder alongside a trail in the winter woods. For me *here* had taken on a much larger meaning: here in the woods, here in Wyoming, here on Earth.

"Nature laughs at me," writes author Sy Safransky. "She's an animal with shining teeth, a mother who doesn't love me. Smoothing her dark skirts, her wild hair blowing free, she asks me if I recognize her. No, I murmur. I'm a city boy."[1] His words spoke my yearnings and my fears, capturing the full extent of the history of my alienation. Not only my life-time but a billion previous years had gone into my sense of homelessness.

For years I had been vaguely familiar with the old theological construct that humankind is separated from God. Christians learn that God and we parted ways at different points in our theological history. We were expelled from the garden, drowned in a deluge, and marked by sin. I had absorbed this idea at some very superficial level. But one morning, with the sound of my feet crunching in new snow and the feel of Arrow's breath puffing against my hand as we took our early walk together, I *felt* that separation. And it was not a separation from the Creator. It was a separation from the living body of the Creator—the Earth.

The pasture was wide and flat and silent, home to the birds who flew over it and the herds of animals that migrated across it, home to the voles that burrowed beneath it and the coyotes who hunted them. But where was my home in such a place? The flat, snowy ground was cold and firm under my feet. I looked down and suddenly saw beneath the white snow cover to the face of the Earth. *A face, a holy, loving face. The Creator's face, the Mother's face.* In that moment of insight, I was shown the first step that would begin to lead me to a sense of home on Earth. The Aborigines admonish us to step softly, because just under the earth are the faces of our unborn children, waiting to sprout from the living body of the infinite. To hold the Earth as a living, sentient, holy mind-body is a vision that can usher us into the realms of relationship and up out of detachment into homecoming.

The Mother speaks ceaselessly and with great expression. That I cannot yet fully decode her words is my lack, not hers. She speaks to me through mountains and trees and

through the great turnings of seasons and tides. She speaks
to me through a deer dying by the side of the road and
through a tiny chipmunk born into bondage and exuberance
all at the same time. She speaks to me of her many, many
gifts to me, gifts that can help me travel through difficult
times, difficult passages. Reminding me through endless cy-
cles of winters, summers, births, and deaths that change is
no accident but a constant in and of time, Earth assures me
that the tools have been given, and given lovingly and with
great tenderness, to ease me and all the rest of my living relations along the journey of transition and change. And by
including me among those so gifted, she assures me that I
do, indeed, belong to her.

Huddled under the covers at my neighbor's house, I
took a moment to breathe fully, expanding my chest and
stomach like a heavy balloon. My return to Wyoming had
signaled the end of life as I knew it in Oregon. My feelings
of isolation from the wilds of Wyoming and from Earth herself had been, in part, exacerbated by the transition process
my move had ignited—a process that sends us catapulting
into a world of inner alienation as we wait for our world to
right itself. In the season of dark grace that had come upon
me in my return to the Rockies, I had projected my inner
isolation out to my physical world and had been gifted with
great insights and understanding about change and homecoming. The house fire was now calling to me from the
inside out, heralding a new turning of seasons in my life, offering me a chance to raise the bar of consciousness in my
world and step up to the next level of awareness.

Something inside me, an emotion tight and holding, let
go with the soft caress of air. And I understood that the
mountains and the wild animals who lived there had placed

in my unknowing hands many precious fragments, many bits and shards of stories and of magical days and nights accumulated over the past three years since my exodus from Oregon. Change was upon me again, but the tools to forge out of the change a blessing instead of a curse were at my fingertips. *Weave the pieces*, Elk whispered to me. *Find the meaning. Find your way home. Again.*

3

Elk Dreaming

*We invite you . . . to cast aside your preconceptions and enter, with us, a
magical world where all things are connected to you, and you are
connected to all things. . . . We see the minerals, the plants, and the
animals as servants of man. We have forgotten that they can be teachers
as well; that they can open us to ideas and emotions that have been
locked from the human heart for too long a time.*
—Sun Bear, *The Medicine Wheel*

"If you really want to know something, look at it again,"
writes Dr. Carl Hammerschlag, psychiatrist and storyteller. "Whenever you see something important, you can
see it from another perspective if you step out of the ordinary and look again. When you can see from an extraordinary perspective, you will know that there is spirit in
everything."[1]

The days and weeks immediately following the fire were
marked by times of near-total numbness in my life. Like
a finger that goes momentarily dead after having been

smacked with a hammer, I felt as though the blow of the fire had pummeled all of me into a kind of vague, senseless pulp. In those first weeks, I struggled to come to terms with all that had ended in my life and to seek what meaning the endings had for me. But as the days and weeks passed and the reconstruction of my house slowly began, I was over-taken with a sense of aimlessness and disconnection that was staggering in its proportions. I had entered what author and teacher William Bridges calls "the fallow zone" in his in-sightful book *Transitions*.

The fallow zone is an uncomfortable land between end-ings and new beginnings where we lie, after the flames have died, like a seed unsprouted in charred ground. But as a "between-time" it is also a rich country where the veils be-tween this realm and the mystery realms are thinnest. The in-between zone is a place in which we can explore the spiritual, numinous landscapes of life, a place where our in-tuition and gut senses are fine-tuned and buzzing. Lost in the fallow zone, I realized the time was ripe for me to "look again," to step out of the ordinary into the extraordinary realms, and I decided to turn my attention upon Elk.

Elk had come to me in the late night hours after the fire. Elk had also been coming into my life for almost a decade, in a series of what I had thought were unrelated fragments. It was time to pull the fragments together and read the story Elk was writing in my life. The story, I knew, would have relevance to me in the wake of the fire, and my inquiry into my relationship with Elk would be a part of my transitional journey.

Traditionally the image of fire is closely related to the Phoenix bird, who rises up victoriously from the ashes of ruin. But the elk had become a more meaningful symbol for me of victory over hardship. This "victory" elk of mine was a bull with an enormous rack of antlers, standing with his head dipped down in meadow grass. I did not know him as a living elk. Rather, his image was from a photograph I had seen twelve years before. It had shocked me and remained embedded in my very bone marrow, because behind the elk raged a wall of fire reaching more than 150 feet into the sky. The photo had been taken during the great Yellowstone fire of 1988, which was of immense personal significance to me.

In the summer of 1988, I had vacationed again in Jackson Hole. It was a glorious trip, traveling with my then boyfriend, Mike. Our days were spent hiking, rafting, and seeking out the wild animal neighbors that lived beneath the stunningly clear Teton skies. To the north in Yellowstone, some lightning fires were kicking up, but it didn't seem to be anything serious. We watched the gray plumes of smoke rise over the Yellowstone Valley fifty miles away and did not give the fire a second thought. On our last day in Jackson Hole, we hiked up to Taggert Lake, a tiny, sparkling jewel of water surrounded by tart-smelling pines and studded with ducks. I rested blissfully on a large flat rock while Mike pulled his camera out of the case to take a picture of me. The afternoon was delicious, and I luxuriated in the joy of being in the Tetons again—the one place on Earth I had always felt was my soul's true home. *Home. On this rock, in this place, beneath these mountains, I am home.*

It was the last photo on Mike's role of film. I pulled myself up, rested my neck in my hand, and smiled up at him. A tiny squirrel barked fiercely at me from a pine tree. As the camera lens clicked, I felt the lump for the first time. It was a hard kernel, like a peanut, nestled under my collarbone and pressing insistently against the side of my hand. My mouth went dry. Eight months before, a cancerous tumor had been removed from the floor of my mouth. My doctors' hope and expectation had been that the malignancy had not traveled. Once a month for eight months, my doctors would run their fingers along my jaw and upper neck, searching for swollen lymph nodes. They had never found any.

But I could not remember their ever checking farther down my neck to the lymph nodes buried like a string of pearls inside the hollow of my collarbone. Only when I tilted my neck for the photo did the fat, hardened little mass extrude from the secrecy of its protective bone cave and reveal itself to me. I pressed the lump. It pressed back. I called Mike over to feel it. Our smiles burned away like fog in sunlight. We walked back down the trail in utter silence. The next morning, still silent, we broke camp and left Jackson Hole. To the north, unknown to us, the fire in Yellowstone exploded as we drove out of the valley.

As I fought my own inner firestorm back in the suburbs of California in the days to come, I felt a deep connection to those fires that were raging states away from me in Yellowstone Park. I was a sister to those flames, having been taken by fire on the very same day and within fifty miles of the same place. Although the cancer had been smoldering inside me for a long time, it did not ignite in my life until the day that I felt its hardness beside the small mountain lake. Yellowstone, too, had been smoldering but did not ignite until the day I left the parks. I felt as though I had started the Yellowstone fires by pressing my hand to my neck.

Weeks later, wading through a medical quagmire of grim statistics and extensive neck surgery, I came across the photo of the bull elk grazing almost meditatively before a gargantuan wall of fire that seemed to reach all the way to heaven. It was one of the first series of photos to come out of the Yellowstone fires and had given me great, immediate comfort. If that elk could face such a consuming fire with peace and graceful adaptation, then perhaps I could at least attempt the same.

The story accompanying the photo had talked about the renewing capacity of fire, about the regrowth that would come in the spring. But mostly it talked reverently about the animals who never panicked before the blaze, who grazed quietly while the fires roared like thundering waterfalls all around them—animals who stepped carefully over charred and smoking ground, seeking food, gathering new nesting materials, quickly rebuilding forest homes.

I had quickly discovered animals and nature in my search for help and healing from cancer. The elk was only one of many animals who touched my life and taught me in those first postcancer years. I realized early in my illness that the world of human wisdom was, sadly, a bastion of repressed creative fire and too small a world in which to live for whatever time I had left to me. My prognosis was near terminal, so there was little hope on my horizon in the human terrain. Doctors shook their heads. My family was terrified. Many old friends were painfully silent in my life or absent. More than once I heard nurses crying outside my hospital room.

Outside of the restrictive realms of human relationship, however, I discovered a wealth of hope, surprise, mystery, acceptance, love, inspiration, and joy—all critical components of healing energy and of simple healthy living. Because I had been enchanted with animals all my life, it was easy for me to welcome them and their wise gifts into my healing journey, much of which I have documented in my previous books. By allowing animals and nature to serve as models, mentors, and teachers in my life, I was vastly increasing the resources and tools available to me to fight the frightful cultural and emotional impoverishment of catastrophic illness.

In the following years, I constantly and thankfully turned to animals and even to memories of animals for strength during my postcancer walk. And the animals generously soothed away much of my fear of illness.

In my early diagnosis, memories of my dog Keesha, who had died of cancer years before, came back to teach me that I could endure anything if I stayed in the present moment, which, of course, was where she lived every minute of her life. Keesha had also taught me through the peaceful unfolding of her death that life need not be clenched in a stranglehold of desperation.

A tiny kitten, whom I named Flora, taught me by surviving feline leukemia that no diagnosis has to be a death sentence and that miracles can and do happen. My debt of gratitude to these animals and to all animals resulted in a complete change in the direction of my life's work. With excitement, passion, and a keen sense of limited time, I put my technical editing career behind me and devoted the next seven years of my life to writing and speaking on behalf of animals, celebrating their profound gifts as teachers and healers.

Some animals would return to me again and again, bringing gifts of healing insight and energy. Elk was one of them. Over and over he came to me in life as well as in spirit and dreams, an enormous wealth of mystery and comfort attending his visits. When I moved from Oregon to Wyoming, home of the largest elk herd in the world, he became an even more powerful presence in my life.

The autumn following my return to Jackson Hole, I was scheduled to fly to Angel Canyon in Utah, to lecture at the Conference on Animals and Spirituality, hosted by Best Friends Animal Sanctuary. Before I left for Utah, I was determined to make a night journey to Teton Park to listen to the bull elk bugling for their cows, an annual event heavily attended by locals. Elk don't bugle so much as they whistle. The sound is very flutelike and delicate. The gruntings that follow on the edge of the elk song are primordial and deep. The cow elk answer with barks, and everything is accompanied by the sound of animals running: elk bulls running off competitors, cows crashing through the brush to get away from overly aggressive suitors, whole herds of elk trotting across meadows and highways.

I packed my traveling bags in the early evening and hurried off into the park with Lee to find an elk or two before I had to leave town. We searched from one end of the park highway to the other, stopping along turnouts to listen in the darkness. No elk. Not a one. It was late, and I had simply not allowed enough time to hike out into the meadows. Giving up hope as a tiny sliver of moon climbed high into the night sky, we turned toward home. One last time I asked Lee to pull over and roll down the windows.

And I heard it—clear and strong, the notes beginning low and then climbing up to end in a high-pitched, bell-like song, reaching to the stars. It was the first time I had heard the sound in a year. The hair rose along my neck and arms, flooding me with a sense of mystery and excitement. Nothing is as ancient as that sound, nor as compelling. I strained to take the notes in, to understand them somehow, to absorb them.

Suddenly I heard a clattering sound, like thousands of pebbles falling on pavement. It was a herd of cow elk, and from the sound of it, they were hurrying down the empty highway directly toward our car. My heart started pounding with the reverberation of the hoofbeats. A sea of restless elk was near to breaking over us. We sat still and stunned as the cows reached us and surrounded our car, snapping the twigs along the side of the road and snorting in the dark. In the dim light of a small moon, I couldn't see them well, but my ears were full of them. They milled around the car, uncertain where to go, so close I could smell them, musty and fresh and female. The car windows were open, so when the bugling sounded again—this time directly out the right window and about thirty feet from my ear—it fairly filled up the car, like river water pouring into a hollow jug.

The sound's effect on me was instant and commanding. I wanted to pull off the confines of polar fleece and underclothes and hiking boots and fling myself naked from the car into the midst of the elk. My bare feet on the highway would clatter like hoofbeats, and I would suck in gulps of black night air and snort them out in an agitated bark. The song ran up my back as cold and stimulating as an icicle. *Brhuuiiiieee! Brrruuhhhwheeee!* The elk sang in a voice hot and insistent. I fidgeted in the car, my ears prickling and my hands working the door handle. The *sound!* All around me cows barked and grunted and rushed. Now the trumpeting sounded on the other side of the car. Then again, just to the front. I put my head back on the seat and felt tears streaming down my cheeks. No suitor had ever called to me that way. Not in a voice so utterly male, so completely confident, so urgent. Emotions raced through me. I felt as if I could ride the love call of the elk up to the very stars. At the same time, I felt terribly alone, an unwelcome spectator to this savage and glorious dance.

Too soon the elk hurried off with his cows into the sage-brush and pines. The crunching of hooves receded, and the call of the bull became as muted and distant as the fall breeze. He was at home with his cows, and I was at home in a box of aluminum and rubber and plastic. I envied him, and I missed him.

The next morning I boarded a plane for Utah. One of the workshops, on shamanic journeying with animals, particularly caught my eye, and I signed up immediately. The instructor was Dr. Susan Keiraleyn, a psychologist from Oregon who has studied shamanic traditions with healers in Nepal and Belize and uses them with her clients to the near exclusion of traditional psychotherapeutic interventions. She claims that journeying works much better and brings insight and transformation on a significantly deeper level.

Within an hour a roomful of us were taking meditative journeys to meet with animal spirits. At first we paired up and journeyed on behalf of each other, because Keiraleyn claimed that the spirit world listened most attentively when you came to bring a message back for someone else. So we carried questions given us by our partners and presented them respectfully to whatever animal spirit showed up to speak with us. When it was time for us to journey on our own behalf, I followed the instructions to find an imagined entrance into the world beneath the surface of the Earth. This spiritual realm is called the lower world and is the place where animal guides wait for us. I let myself follow a tunnel down, down through the dark toward the light of an open summer meadow surrounded by pine trees and singing birds. The smell of flowers and new grass surrounded me. An animal was waiting for me in the woods, and as it moved into the light, I could see that it was a large bull elk.

I sucked in my breath and heard again the bugling call I remembered from my car window. I could hear the feet of my spirit elk snapping thin twigs. From his head rose a huge, six-pointed rack of antlers. His neck was thick and bulging with muscles. Every inch of his body rippled with strength and vigor. He approached me with a look of serenity and composure in his topaz eyes. In response my muscles relaxed and my breath softened. In the background I could hear the swift pounding of Keiraleyn's drum, framing the journey and putting a precise limit to the extent of it. When the drum stopped, then sounded again with three hard beats, I was to return to my world at the top of the tunnel. Not wanting to waste a moment of this precious traveling time, I hurried to greet the elk.

Hello! You are so beautiful! Do I know you? I held out my hand, and he sniffed my open palm.

He snorted. His mouth did not move, and I heard his communication only in my mind. *I came to you only two nights ago. Do you remember? You wanted to join us.*

Yes, oh yes! I remember. It was magnificent. Your song touched my soul. Why have you come to me today?

We would have you know that you came back to the Teton mountains because we called you there. We could not keep you safe in your body any longer where you were, and so we called to you. Our gift to you is to guard your health. Do not kill us. Do not hang our heads on your wall. Do not eat elk meat. Honor us by visiting us and talking with us. Honor all animals, every moment of every day. The drum went quiet. The elk looked me full in the face. Then I heard three rapid drumbeats, calling me away. I threw my arms around the elk and thanked him as earnestly as I could before turning to run across the meadow and up the tunnel to the other world.

There are older and wiser teachers on this planet than us humans. "Native people think of minerals, plants, and animals as all having certain powers," writes Sun Bear. "We refer to these other beings as our relations and as our totems. We know that each species has a protector spirit. When we need help we pray for that protector spirit to help us. We see the universe as having both a visible and invisible world. . . . The invisible world is that of the spirit beings who are placed here to oversee everything on the planet. These spirits work with the Creator and they are available to help humanity."[2]

From long before I knew of Native traditions, I saw the world as Sun Bear did. Because of this, I took the message from Elk seriously. When I returned home, I looked up Elk in my numerous animal symbol books, all of which presented Elk as the teacher of stamina and endurance. Another quality of Elk is his ability to conserve energy and to pace himself.

Throughout my life I have taken on too much and tried to complete tasks too soon. My energy flows in fits and bursts, and my frenetic schedule has often left me open to exhaustion and illness. No wonder Elk has stayed with me, bringing reminders of how to maintain my health through endurance and pacing. Even with Elk's steady guidance, however, it has taken me years to slow down intentionally, to shift my pace to allow myself some much-needed rest.

After the house fire, Lee and I and our animal family spent two weeks with neighbors before finding a rental house two miles away from our house. Factory-built and called a "prefab" by everyone around here, it was musty and tired-looking, but it was close to home. Every morning I would walk Arrow and Strongheart up the road to our barn and care for Fashion, Aurora, and Polani. Those January mornings were the coldest of the year, the mercury often dropping to twenty-five or more below zero. It is a cold that instantly freezes your eyelashes and catches in your throat with a rasping cough.

One morning as I turned up the drive toward the barn, the morning light was just beginning to touch the tree trunks and the snow trails, wrapping everything in an ethereal pink glow the color of rose petals. Walking up our long driveway, I looked out behind the barn, where the mixed aspen and pine forest looked like an image from a dream. All the trees were shimmering white with glassy coats of hoarfrost. Each breath of morning air sent down cascades of gleaming snow crystals from limbs and shrubs—hundreds of them—pouring like frothy, dancing waterfalls from an entire forest of trees. I quickly put hay out for the animals and stopped, spellbound, to watch the heart-stopping beauty in front of me.

As the first rays of sun reached me, I saw a movement in the aspens, just above the pasture. From out of the forest of cascading light, a six-point bull elk stepped onto the trail to our barn. Strongheart and Arrow saw him instantly and erupted into static barks, which echoed off the hillside like harsh gunfire. Then, just as suddenly, they sat down in a posture of absolute alertness and went completely quiet, watching him. The elk stopped, looked directly at me and the dogs, and waited. I could see the frosted hairs on his back and the puffs of white breath coming from his nose. We looked at each other for a long, long time, until the cold made me move. I finished shoveling a pile of manure out of the barn and went out back to fill up the metal watering trough. The donkeys were so short, I had to shovel snow and sawdust into a little mound by the trough or they couldn't reach the water. While I worked, the bull watched me, not moving a foot from where he stood. The dogs stayed at the pasture fence, their eyes never leaving him. Slapping strands of loose hay from my coat, I called my dogs, put a long lead on Strongheart, whose response to "come" is less than sterling, and started for home. I could feel the bull's eyes tickling the back of my head as we left.

The next morning, when the dogs and I rounded the corner of our street on the way to our property, I saw what looked like a huge bush waving in the air by the side of the road. It was a set of enormous antlers. The bull elk had followed us down from the barn and was now taking up residence at a horse pasture just a few houses up from my rental place. The dogs and I circled around him, coming within fifteen feet of where he stood munching on a hay flake while two horses watched him, ears up and nostrils flaring. The bull never so much as batted an eye at any of us.

For several weeks I saw him daily. He would be either behind my barn in the meadow or somewhere on my block. Neighbors took lots of video movies of him and spoke in breathless excitement of our newest "neighbor," and I hoped with all digits crossed that their enthusiastic acceptance of him would continue as the novelty of his presence wore off. I called my friend, animal communicator Sharon Callahan, and told her about this wonderful being who had stepped like magic out of the forest. From the moment I saw him, I felt he had come to me. Sharon said, "Yes, he tells me he is there for you and will stay as long as you need him."

He became "my" elk, not in any sense of ownership but out of the very special connection I felt to him. He was my in-the-flesh elk, who also held the space for the symbolic and totemic aspects of Elk that continued to weave power-fully into the fabric of my life. I would put out offerings for him: ritual offerings of tobacco and cornmeal, and friend-ship offerings of apples and hay. I prayed for his health and safety in a valley of hunters and sportsmen, as I imagined he held vigil for mine.

The terrible morning I will never forget came in early February and began with the frenzied whine of snowmobiles whizzing outside my rental house. The dogs erupted into barking fits, and I ran outside in house slippers to see my elk galloping past the side of the house, tongue hanging, sweat flying, muscled legs lunging through drifts of snow five feet deep while snowmobiles charged after him with the whine of gigantic wasps. It was Wyoming Game and Fish, come to run my elk back to the federal refuge, come at the request of a neighbor who no longer felt like sharing an occasional flake of hay, who was afraid of that big rack of antlers, which sometimes aimed in warning toward his horses. Come to put the wild animals back where too many thought they belonged—on a fenced feeding ground.

I screamed as the snowmobiles flew by me, and they stopped. Plowing through snow that went nearly to my waist, I watched in horror as the two men pulled out rifles and loaded them. My hands and voice shook out of con-trol as I asked them what they were doing. The rifles, they claimed, were tranquilizer guns, and they were going to shoot the elk, load him in a horse trailer, and drive him to the refuge. I turned my head to see my elk far, far away like a brown dot in the snowfields, still lunging, leaping, falling in his frenzied dash to escape the predatory rush of the snowmobiles. In films I had seen elk running from wolves, and they ran to the fast but measured step of a heartbeat, pacing, pacing. Never had I seen one running like this one—in a mindless, heartbreaking panic. It was unnatural. It was hideous. Bile rushed into my mouth with a taste like hot gasoline.

I did not believe the men with the guns. I dragged my-self to the front of the sleds and stood on the runners. "How do I know that's a tranquilizer gun?" I asked. "I think you are going to kill him." The taller man with silver hair looked at me with thinly disguised disgust. He snapped open the gun to reveal a dart, then looked expectantly at me. I stood there in the deep snow, shaking all over with cold and with a helpless sense of dread that turned my limbs to jelly and my stomach into a volcano. I felt sick and weak and hopeless. I could not stop them. All I could do was to speak on behalf of my elk. I cleared my throat and croaked out a plea: "This elk has been a good neighbor. I've seen him with the dogs on the street, and he has never hurt one. Not one. He has been far more patient with all of us than we deserve. The horses respect him and stay away. He belongs here more than any of us. This is his home. Don't hurt him. Please, I beg you." My voice cracked and melted into streaming tears. "Please don't hurt him."

The men turned away, embarrassed. "We'll do our best." The engines roared to life, and they were gone. Sobbing, I dragged myself back to the house. The bull had been there for me, and I could not help him. The neighborhood would not help him. For a full year, I never found out what had happened to my beautiful, magical guardian, because I was too afraid to ask. I assumed that he had died, because an animal run hard to the point of exhaustion fares poorly when tranquilized. Only while writing this chapter did I inadvertently learn about an elk who had been brought to the elk refuge last year—a six-point bull who came in the back of a horse trailer, drunk with tranquilizer darts, pulled out of our subdivision. He did just fine, the refuge manager told me. Just fine.

It was no small wonder that Elk in dream, in symbol, and in body had come to me after the fire. Houses are not constructed in fits and starts nor rebuilt overnight. Reconstruction of a home is a task that requires steady pacing and considerable endurance, as anyone who has ever undertaken a building project can tell you. Pacing, endurance, stamina, and strength—these, too, are the gifts that carry us through difficult changes. Transitions challenge us to our very core, demanding the full complement of our time and energy. Without the virtues of endurance and pacing embodied in the wisdom of Elk, changes weigh much more heavily upon us.

After my bull elk was taken away, I returned to my investigation of the symbolic meaning of Elk and discovered that in Native American tradition, bull elk are thought to have awesome seductive powers. Elk Dreamers—men who through dreams and visions claimed the bull elk as their totem animals—were said to be powerful seducers with a compelling, almost hypnotic ability to enchant women. Their flutes could wield the mysterious power of the bugling elk, and their love songs were said to be almost impossible to deny. Misused, this power over women could turn back upon the dreamers and hurt or even kill them. The stamina and endurance of Elk extended into intimate arenas, too. Surely, I thought, almost squirming in discomfort at this aspect of Elk, this had nothing to hold for me. Intimacy, romance, and passion were just about—no, not just about; they *were*—the last things on my mind. I brushed aside the thoughts and focused my will where I suspected it would do the most immediate good: fire cleanup.

4

Salt Ceremony

From my own experience of Neo-pagan rituals,
I have come to feel that they have another purpose—
to end, for a time, our sense of human alienation
from nature and from each other. Rituals have
the power to reset the terms of our universe
until we find ourselves suddenly and truly home.
—Margot Adler

I try to walk each day as a prayer. . . .
—David Bearclaw Abrams

I hung the square of suet in the holder by the fence and went back to the house with my coffee cup to sit by the window and wait. In a moment a crow came hopping down the fence rail, bobbed his head three times, bounced up and down on the railing, fluffed his feathers, and began whacking chips out of the frozen fat with his bill. I could set a clock by his arrival and had begun looking forward to this simple, early morning ritual at my rental house.

Observing animals over the course of my lifetime had made me deeply respectful of the practice of ritual and ceremony—even those of the smallest sort like that enacted by my early morning crow. In the lives of animals, I saw daily and seasonal rituals that evoked in me a deep sense of the sacred and of mystery. This is what ritual is: an invitation into the sacred, a bridge constructed between the landscapes of mystery and our everyday world. Seeking to deepen my connection with my spiritual self during the slow, slogging months of postfire fallow time, I turned my attention to the practice of ceremony.

Every evening I watch my dog Arrow circle and circle on the carpet like a determined top and finally plop down with a deep grunt—her bedtime ceremony complete for the night. Each time she performs this ritual in my presence, I feel my own body release a portion of the day's concerns, and I feel myself move into a different mode of being. Through her simple ceremony, my own heart settles and my body begins moving into its own place of evening rest. Arrow and many other animals teach me that rituals needn't be elaborate ceremonies to move one into sacred, transformative space.

I cannot know what Arrow's simple evening ceremony means to her nor how it feels in her body and her heart. I don't believe that her rituals take her into sacred space, because I believe that animals live in sacred space all the time. It seems to me that animals, unlike humankind, have never left holy ground—that place of unquestioned trust and communion with life and living. Perhaps her small and steady ceremony simply acknowledges a relationship with Creation that is her natural home.

Every year a pair of robins make their nest on top of my front-porch light fixture, returning to my house within the same two-week period in the early spring. They construct the cup-sized nest with twigs from the aspens out front and always line it thickly with Strongheart's signature white hair. Around the robins' comings and goings, I have established a series of welcoming rituals for them of my own. As soon as the snow begins melting, I start brushing Strongheart out on the front lawn, knowing the birds will be looking for his hair. Once the first twig appears on my front deck, all of us stop using the front door and start coming and going from the garage so that the new parents can have some privacy. When I see the robins begin sitting for long hours in the nest, I begin my spring prayers for the safety of these new lives who swim inside a liquid sea, encased in sky-blue eggs. The ritual of the robins' annual return ushers in a special time for me in early spring, sending my thoughts toward new beginnings and new births, not only of birds and babies but of my own ideas and dreams for the coming season.

In the fall I discover the nut piles of squirrels stashed at the bases of trees lining the path of my afternoon walk. High up in the limbs, territorial squirrels bark fiercely at me, and I realize that their ritual fall harvest and gathering—like our own fall garden harvests—signifies the coming cold season, when all green growing things will sleep in darkness. It is time, then, to prepare for the hard lessons of winter ahead. As soon as I see the nut piles, I head for the phone and begin my search for wood for the heat stove. The squirrel ceremony sings to me of the coming season of introspection, in which weather will force me not only inside the house but inside myself. I touch the interior ground around me, searching for the harvest I've sown the previous summer in my inner garden. Some years the crop is richer and more plentiful than others. It is from this crop of life and story and dreams that I will feed my soul in the coming six months.

"We often think of ritual as belonging to the realm of religion," write Renee Beck and Sydney Metrick, "but in fact, rituals are an integral part of nature and of our daily lives. Animals have ritualized ways of defining and defending their territory. . . . Animals and birds often have elaborate courting and mating rituals."[1]

One autumn evening Lee and I drove to the top of nearby Signal Mountain to watch the sunset. From down below us on the valley floor, a breath of evening breeze caught the sound of bugling elk gathered in a complete circle ringing the mountain and carried it up to us. Muted by the distance and transformed by the sheer number of trumpeting animals, the sound was a rich symphony of exuberance, sweet and magical in the quiet evening air. It was impossible to hear the music and not be transported into a place of peace and stillness. So deeply did this experience touch my heart that I have made it a ritual of my own now to journey up to the mountaintop each fall and listen to the orchestra of elk flutes in a circle below me.

Late one winter night, I awoke to sounds unlike any I'd ever heard coming through my open window. Even though the night temperatures in winter dip below freezing, I always sleep with the bedroom window ajar. At two in the morning, I was startled out of deep sleep by a strange noise that sounded like a child making a high-pitched, loud squeal through a long metal pipe. I lay there in the dark, covers pulled up to my chin, listening. There it came again, hollow, high, echoing against the hill behind the house. All around the house, the night was saturated in the noiseless wonder of deep winter silence, a clear, empty stillness that embraces every breath of noise and magnifies it and throws it back out into the blue-black air. In the fog of half sleep, I thought, *This is the sound of stars. The stars are calling out tonight.*

I pulled myself out of bed, crept over to the window, and turned the crank to open it wider. The moon was a silver splinter, and I could see nothing. The squeal came again, followed by the sound of breaths—big, puffing exhales that ended with a snort, then a crash and a clacking sound, almost like wind chimes banging together in a fierce blow. *Bull elk,* I thought. No longer bugling but pushing out a heart sound like the muted song of a humpback whale, calling across oceans of time and space. The rut was long gone, but late in winter, on this night, the bulls reenacted the ritual and evoked the mating energy. Emotion carries ritual and gives it strength. And so the voices of the elk, bleating and powerful, carried into the night air and settled over the pasture, extending long, blue fingers to me inside my window. I heard the muffled barks of a small herd of cow elk, calling from far away. Already their babies rolled and swam in their bellies like spinning planets, planted there months ago. I pressed my hands to my belly—to a womb that has remained waiting, hopeful, and empty for all of my life—and I returned to the warm covers of my bed, my body wrapped in a shiver of energy that emanated from my stomach and reached in a soft caress up my spine. The clashing duel of the elk, vigorous and exciting, went on for a long time, the sharp, precise sound ringing across the snowfield and following me back into sleep, where I dreamed of infant elk curled like tiny, umbilical-wrapped gifts in fields of yellow and red flowers.

When my good friend Janet and her daughter Meredith were visiting me one afternoon by the shores of a nearby creek, we watched, spellbound, as her chocolate lab, Carob, encircled us in stones he gathered from under the water. "He's making a medicine wheel around us," Janet observed delightedly. This was neither the first nor the last time Carob celebrated a small gathering of women in this way. Janet calls Carob her spirit dog and is always happy to tell the story of his ritual gifts of circle casting. Often he brings up rocks from the very bottom of a stream to place in his circle, dunking and gasping in his efforts to enclose us in sacred space. His work that afternoon on our behalf caused us to view our visit with one another through different eyes. Carob's stone ceremony enabled us to see more clearly the dignity and power and mystery of women gathering together for personal sharing and support.

A reader told me about a women's spirituality workshop she was facilitating. A young female wolf was in attendance. "As we got ready to close for the evening, she sang for us a wolfy wildsong that reached the wilderness inside each one of us and for magical moments gave us back our natural selves to celebrate and to honor." Like Carob, this wolf brought the magic of ritual to the moment.

What is the effect of an altered state brought about by ritual? "Rituals and symbols can provide the structure by which life experiences yield new meaning," writes Dr. Carl Hammerschlag. "They help rediscover things you may need to see differently. . . . It is through ritual that we separate our ordinary selves from our extraordinary possibilities and create the sacred time necessary to address important questions with the attention they deserve. . . . Ritual can guide us through crises by anchoring us in our spiritual truth."[2]

I have found my thoughts during ritual slipping into a quieter, instantly more reflective space. From this safe and mysterious ground, I see the world through softer, more trusting eyes. I have come to view the seasonal changes of the year as ceremonies of a sort also. Because autumn is my favorite season, I am particularly moved by her season's rituals. Last fall I watched the lemon-yellow autumn leaves on my aspen trees flutter to the ground like a flock of small golden birds. I ran outside to let the cold wind drive the crisp leaves down in a cascade over my face and arms and breathed in the melancholy taste of the season. In the flock of leaves, I caught brief glimpses of the previous year— its successes and failures—in moments of joy and regret spilling onto the ground, to be covered soon by the blanket of winter snow, the snows that would symbolically put the year and all it had contained for me to bed.

Later that week I saw a flock of migrating cranes pass over my house like the outline of some great, gray ship floating slowly on a sea of deep blue mountain air. The season had called them, and it had called me. Who hasn't witnessed a fall migration of birds and felt called to join in that ancient, formal journey?

Observing the winter hair come in heavy and thick on my dogs as early as late August is another natural ritual that marks a time for me to begin preparing for winter. As I run my hands through Strongheart's unbelievably dense white fur, like a polar bear pelt, I am called by the season to put away the garb of summer and to begin reflecting on the months of cold whiteness ahead of me—months that will beckon me closer to home and hearth and winter dreams.

These natural ceremonies—of leaves falling, of coats thickening, of spring branches budding and blossoming, of fruit ripening on the vines—when observed and marked by an expression of humility, awareness, and awe, take us to that "extraordinary" place of which Hammerschlag writes. They offer us an unscheduled, unexpected moment to stop, to reflect, to feel, and to view the world and our lives through our spirit eyes. Ceremonies we create ourselves have a similar effect, taking us to these spirit realms by our own hand and in our own time.

Although I have believed in the power of ritual for years, it was a long time before I ever participated in any personal ceremony of my own. Creating comfortable ceremonial space on my own eluded me, as it was not a part of my familial or Christian tradition, and my self-taught rituals have often been contained and small, performed with a faltering sense of embarrassment. Simply put, I have not been "at home" with ceremony. Then I met David, a Cherokee teacher living in a mountain valley not far from mine.

He sat in the back row of the first presentation on animals and healing that I gave for my local hospital. A variety of nurses and health-care workers were in attendance. The medical doctors were conspicuously absent. I remember his black hat and his long gray ponytail and the earring with a silver feather on it. He sat, arms crossed, and watched me with a look that I could not read. Interest? Politeness? After I finished my lecture, he approached me and handed me a business card that read "David Bearclaw Abrams," with a post office box and phone number listed below. He thumbed through a copy of my book, nodded to me, and left. I could not forget his face.

The next time I spoke at the hospital, it was again to medical staff members. I was excited to see "Bearclaw," arms folded, again in the back row. At the close of my talk, someone asked me, based on my enchantment with animals and my belief in their gifts as healers and teachers, how I felt about eating meat. I answered that I was torn about the topic. I said that I killed many bugs and weeds in the harvesting of my potatoes and vegetables each fall, and I could not imagine that the Creator cared less for his bugs and weeds than for his cows and chickens. Living things died so that I might live and eat.

David raised his hand suddenly, then rose to his feet, nodding to me. "I will tell you this: You are one of the old teachers. Everything you have said is true. Ant or cow, it is all life, and it is all *one* life." He held up his finger and marked the air. "One life. There is no difference." He sat down, his eyes still hooked to mine. When I was finished and all the questions had been answered and my books signed and sold, he was gone. This time I dug out his business card, and in the following week, I called him. "I would like to take you to lunch and talk with you, if that would be OK." I felt awkward. I didn't know anything about him, and he did not make the conversation easy. There was a long pause.

"What for?" He sounded reserved, or was it suspicious?

"I'm not sure." I was starting to stutter. "I just thought that maybe you and I might have some work to do together . . ." My voice faltered and trailed off into a silence as uncomfortable and pinched as a too-tight pair of shoes.

"I'll have lunch with you, but lunch will be on me. Come on down to the hospital and meet me in the chapel at noon on Wednesday. Will that work for you?" It would.

I don't know what I expected, but based on our phone conversation, I did not expect David Bearclaw Abrams to be as warm and conversational as he turned out to be. He came into the small chapel dressed in kitchen garb—checkered cook pants, a white shirt, and a hospital ID badge. The hat was gone, but the ponytail and the earring were still there, and I noticed a stone and bear claw necklace around his throat. He took my hand warmly and escorted me into the cafeteria for coffee. I learned that he worked in the purchasing department and that he lived in a mountain valley outside of Jackson Hole, about fifty miles away. I guessed his age to be midfifties, but his face seemed timeless in its composure and kindliness. His eyes were dark and his lips full and easily pulled into a smile. There was a touch of the southern states in his words, and his voice itself was very quiet, almost a whisper.

We returned to the chapel to talk, and he opened our conversation with, "I was waiting for your call." I knew he was telling the truth because when I had called his house and asked his wife, Star, if I could speak with him, she answered, "Is this Susan?" For the next hour and a half, David shared with me pieces of his life and work, but mostly he shared his spiritual vision. "I try to walk each day as a prayer. Work here is what I do to keep a roof over my head, but only to the extent that it does not interfere with my spiritual life and with teaching." I learned that David—a mixed-blood Cherokee—carried a medicine pipe, was a Sun Dancer in the Lakota tradition, and had been taught by a Shoshone medicine man named John. He had built his own log cabin and put a medicine wheel and sweat lodge on his property, where he held community sweats regularly. Once a year he hosted a Cherokee Green Corn Dance ceremony on the Greys River. Every July he danced at the Sun Dance tree in Colorado for four days.

The more he talked, the more excited I became. For years I had dreamed of finding a teacher in the indigenous traditions. Native practitioners of these ancient ways still know how to speak to the Earth and hear the Earth answer back. To hold in my heart even a tiny part of the wisdom of tribal vision was to hold another key that could help guide me out of planetary exile.

If you were to speak to an indigenous person—any of the tribal people, or "first people," still living the ways of an ancient culture—you would not likely find any stories of exile on Earth. Tribal creation stories explain exactly where people belong here and why they belong here. "We think of ourselves not as human beings first, but as sons and daughters . . . tribesmen and neighbors. It is this dense web of relationship and the meanings which they give to life which satisfies the needs [that] really matter to us."[3]

Over thousands of years, tribal people the world over have watched animals and the living world around them, amassing a vast, universal wisdom about Earth and her many, many children. "Everything was possessed of personality, only differing from us in form," writes Chief Luther Standing Bear. "Knowledge was inherent in all things. The world was a library and its books were the stones, leaves, grass, brooks, and the birds and animals that shared, alike with us, the storms and blessings of Earth. We learned to do what only the student of nature ever learns, and that was to feel beauty. We never railed at the storms, the furious winds, and the biting frosts and snows. To do so intensified human frailty, so whatever came, we adjusted ourselves . . . without complaint. This appreciation enriched Lakota existence. Life was vivid and pulsating; nothing was casual or commonplace."[4]

When I read the words of tribal people, of first people, I feel the truth boiling up from the page like strong, nourishing broth. It is a tonic of ceremony, ritual, and tradition, and I asked David if he would share with me some of what he knew. I told him that my spirit had been searching for these teachings for a long, long time.

I knew nothing about the pipe; the sweat lodge, or *inipi*, ceremony; the medicine wheel traditions; or the thanksgiving ceremonies of the Corn Dance and Sun Dance. And I wanted to know everything, and I wanted to know it all in that moment. Once again, as it had happened so many times since the writing of *Animals as Teachers and Healers*, my book had brought me a precious gift. It had brought me to David, or David to me. My body was fairly shaking with emotion when I asked David if he took on students. "Sometimes," he said. "But you need to be serious. I don't have time to waste."

A month ahead, he told me, was the August Green Corn Dance festival, a four-day event of dancing and prayers. "Start there," he said. "See how it feels. We'll have *inipis*; there will be pipe ceremonies, the drums, and the dance. Some of it will speak to you, and some of it won't. We can go from there." Ceremony, I learned from David, is how we give back to the Earth a bit of the endless abundance we receive from her. In ceremony we give what is ours to give: our voices, our prayers, our dances, our ritual practices.

Many of the ceremonies to which David exposed me

that summer were traditional ones. Pipe ceremonies and sweat ceremonies have been handed down over hundreds— perhaps thousands—of years. In traditional ceremony it is important that the ceremony be done in an exact way, as these ceremonies call in very powerful spirit helpers, and it is imperative that these helpers be treated in the appropriate manner. I learned that you do not conduct ceremonies of this kind unless you have been taught by a qualified person who has given you specific authority to do so. But I also learned from David about self-generated ceremonies. Sun Bear, a medicine teacher, defined self-generated ceremonies in this way: "These ceremonies are ones that have come to us in our own visions, dreams, or meditations. Self-generated ceremonies seem most appropriate for people learning about ceremony and their relationship with the Earth. This type of ceremony allows one to have a good framework to which he can add components that come to him in his own intuitive work."[5]

There are as many ways to pray, to offer blessings and gratitude, to seek insight and spirit help, and to celebrate joy as there are humans on the planet. Self-generated ceremony is a ritual we create and prepare out of our own heart. It is not as exacting as traditional ceremony, and it appropriates or steals nothing from another culture. Ceremony is our birthright.

Months later, on the eve of New Year's, I stood with Lee in the snowfields in front of our house. On the ground was an abalone shell filled with twigs and paper bits that would serve as kindling. In our hands were the notes we had written that past hour—letters to ourselves about what we wanted to release in the coming year. We had listed all the qualities that held us back and hurt us in our relationship and in our lives. These were things we did not want to take into a new year with us. And so we placed the letters on the shell and put a match to them and watched it all burn. In the cold starlight, we stood silently until the last ember turned dark. Then we kissed and hugged each other and walked back into the house. For the first time since I'd left Brightstar Farm in Oregon, my new house felt like home. For my tiny New Year's ritual—for the confidence to create it and the faith to perform it—I had David to thank.

My friend Jane called me shortly after my house burned. "Susan," her voice was urgent over the phone, "you simply *must* reclaim your home. You need to walk every inch of ground and sprinkle salt everywhere, saying with each and every step, 'I reclaim this ground for the good.' "

Jane's voice, a soft southern drawl, was as gentle and sweet as jam on biscuits. I thought about all the fear and chaos that had come into my home space with the fire. The firemen, the neighbors, me, and my family all had brought our fears and despair into the now-gutted bulk of my house. Jane made absolute sense. *Yes, a cleansing ritual with salt*, a first step in reclaiming home with a positive intention. Also, a way to symbolically honor the hollowness, the emptiness of the dwelling that was so reminiscent of my own inner house at that particular between-time of my transitional journey.

Assembling the tools for a private ceremony, I felt David's presence close by. The feathers I would use to smudge and purify my house were a gift from him, as was the smudge of finely ground sage and cedar itself and the leather pouch that held it. But more than the ceremonial tools he had gifted to me was the confidence to create and

perform the ritual itself. It was a confidence born and nurtured over time under David's kind and patient supervision
and encouragement.

I put the salt, a candle, the smudge, the raven-tail fan,
and matches in a carry bag. "Ritual is the way we perform
ceremony," David taught me. "In Holy Communion, the
wine and the bread and the passing of them is the ritual.
The ceremony is the emotional vessel that holds all the
ritual. Smoking the pipe is a ritual. The prayers that we send
in the pipe create the ceremony. Rituals allow us the means
to come into the mystery realms of being. When ritual is
done well, with great care, it becomes ceremony. Ritual performed with careless hands and a distracted heart is just a
bunch of 'stuff.' "

I walked to my house. The contractors were gone early,
and the house was vacant and cold. Ice framed the windows,
and a few thin icicle spears hung from the ravaged walls of
the kitchen. I heard my feet, hollow and hard, ring out on
the stripped floorboards of the living room. In the middle
of the room, I took out my treasures. The black feathers on
the raven-tail fan shone like pewter. I put rock salt in a small
bowl and placed it in front of me. Untying the bag that held
the smudging sage and cedar, I accidentally dropped the
contents of the bag onto the floor. Even today, after several
years of learning and practicing, ceremonies for me rarely
go smoothly. I forget, I stumble, I am often less than graceful. But David let me know from the start that intention is
what is most important. "Do you think the Creator cares
more about how you perform or about what is in your heart?
And—do you think the Creator has no sense of humor?"

Lighting the pieces of sage and cedar in an abalone

shell, I cupped the sweet smoke in my hands and poured it over me like water. I used the raven fan to fluff the smoke into the corners of the room, each room, throughout the entire house. Then I picked up the bowl of salt, scattering it through all the rooms and outside around all of the house and grounds. Purification ceremonies are universal traditions among all of Earth's first people. Whoever my ancestors are, they, too, were at one time tribal people. All of us and our humanness were birthed in tribes. I know in my bones that if I could go back far enough, I would find a relative of mine sitting before sweet-smelling smoke or incense, a bowl of water or a flame, and asking for cleansing. And so I joined in ritual with these ancestors, and with every being who has ever asked for cleansing, coming together with the ancient ones across time in a great circle vortex of ceremony.

As I walked the borders of my property, with each step, according to Jane's counsel, I said out loud, "Where my feet step, I reclaim this ground for the good." The salt crystals fell into the snow and vanished. I walked in a circle, following the course of the sun, moving from east to south, to west, and then north. Time slept, and I saw nothing but my feet stepping slowly in front of each other, the bits of salt falling to the ground like snow. The bowl was soon empty, and I walked back to the house. In the woodstove I placed the burning remains of the sage. Then I sat down in the silence. The house was between its end and its rebirth. So was my life. In the comforting moments of respectful silence, I told the Creator that I was making room for whatever was to come to my house and to me. *Not my will but thine.*

"How can we tap into the sustaining dimension that can help us make sense of the events in our lives, and even get through them?" writes Hammerschlag. "Rituals and ceremonies can . . . reconnect us with our spiritual selves."[6] As I had walked the circle in my salt ceremony, my mind stepping out of the confines of intellectual time and into spirit time, I understood through a deeply felt sense in my body that the house fire had created a great world of distance between my home and me. Somehow the salt and the smoke and the healing intention of my small ceremony worked together to spin the first gossamer threads of a supportive embrace between my heart and my home. I let out a great breath, and it hung in the cold air of the empty living room like a soft cloud.

There is great power in the rituals I bring into my life. They bind me to a healing, transforming process that is beyond words. Perhaps it is because the Earth, too, moves in endless ritual and has for billions of years, bringing us this knowledge where it comes at last to rest, sleeping, in our old brain. The seasons, the orbit of Earth around its sun, the tradition of water moving over rock and transforming it slowly and irrefutably, these are rituals—processes that repeat themselves over and over again with Creation's purpose, emotion, and ceremonial precision. These ceremonies of planetary celebration both sustain and miraculously transform life on Earth, all in the same instant.

And so ritual works its way in me, sustaining me yet transforming me at the same time. It is part of the great journey home to our most authentic selves. I mimic my Earth Mother in my calling to ritual, like a child who puts on her mother's clothes and feels the mystery of adulthood creep in for an instant through the fabric. In the same way, I step into ritual and feel for that instant a small bit of the wisdom of mystery creeping through Creation's fabric: a gift that I will try on again and again, until I grow into it. Gathering up the raven fan and the abalone shell, I turned to leave, sustained and calm inside. My living space had been made into sacred ground by claiming it with intention and emotion. The house, no matter who came into its space now, would be held safe and dear. And I knew that the ceremony would hold me in the same way.

I trudged up the snow-covered road with Arrow, my salt ceremony completed. The sense of peace and mystery lingered long after the last scent of sage left me, and I was aware that I was still moving in extraordinary time. Looking back down the road to a home burned beyond recognition, I turned my head up to the aspens. They stood bare and brittle in the icy cold. Through them I imagined that I could hear the gift of my true mother's voice—my Earth Mother—clearly. She whispered softly through naked winter trees, her voice like clattering twigs and cold winter breeze.

She stood in spirit as tall as mountains, an enormous and elusive shadow behind the filter of the tree limbs. Radiantly feminine she stood, wrapped in a cloak of grasses and rivers, her hair made of otters and dragonflies, her hands as delicate as new leaves. Her feet were bare and translucent as a summer sky, her fingers long and narrow like tiny streams of mountain water. *Daughter, my gift to you,* she calls quietly to me, *is in making loss real. Now you have more than a vague, intellectual sense of exile and of change. Now you are a refugee. And, daughter, there will be other losses still to come, other places of no longer belonging before you see your life step onto its new path. Belonging. Belongings. Now your belongings are ashes, so you must find your way to a truer sense of home. You are called to new work: work to reclaim and rebuild* and to celebrate the season of change. The harder work before you is to NOT rebuild. Seek your truest self in the tasks that require your heart and your hands. Find homecoming—not just this house but in your inner houses. Thank you for the sweet smoke and for the purity of the salt. Daughter, follow Elk. Remember him as the Dreamer. He will lead you. Come home.

Poison into Good

Snake ceremonies involved learning to transmute the poisons within the body after being bitten multiple times. Survival of this would then enable the individual to transmute all poisons—physical or otherwise.
—Ted Andrews, *Animal-Speak*

Sympathy for the loss of our home poured in daily and continued for weeks after the fire. "We are so sorry about the house fire." "What rotten luck." "What a terrible thing to happen to anyone." I, too, was still shocked about the event, but as my numbness evaporated, the sharp reality of the hard work in front of me became overwhelmingly clear. The work of rebuilding seemed monumental. The insurance forms were endless, and reconstructing a home in the middle of winter in Wyoming was, during many weeks of hard snow and blinding wind, nearly impossible. As I told myself how enormous a task reclaiming the house was going to be, I sank under the power of my own squelching thoughts. It was as though the fresh new snow load that threatened what remained of our house roof had settled squarely onto my shoulders. I turned to prayer, to quiet morning ceremonies of supplication, and to simply crying in the snowfields for help.

Then one night my prayers brought me a vivid dream: I was back at Brightstar Farm in Oregon, and I discovered a fat, coiled rattlesnake in our backyard. As I approached, she began spewing tiny baby snakes all over the yard. Hundreds of them wiggled into the grass, under the shrubbery, and across the pasture. I hurried the dogs into the house, fearful that they would be poisoned if they accidentally stepped on one.

Awakening with a start, I knew immediately that the dream snake had come to me as a reminder of a very real snake who had crossed my path only two years before. The snake and its message had lived in my journal since our last meeting. But now it was clear to me that the entirety of events that led up to our original meeting had great significance for me as I faced the task of reclaiming my home and, more important, finding the heart and the energy to do it.

My snake adventure began at Best Friends Animal Sanctuary in Utah, where I had finished up a three-day conference on animals and spirituality. Lee had accompanied me, and I decided to show him some pictographs that I had seen in the canyon.

The year before I had followed Kate, a guide from Best Friends, up along the crimson-and-pink canyon face until we came to a place where desert shrubs and juniper trees kissed an ancient piece of smooth, shaded stone wall. The canyon itself is a wonder of a place, its rock walls running a color spectrum of deep red to blushing pink and deep rose. The forms of the rock are rounded, coiling, pulsating. Inside the

shaded glens, I have often felt that I am inside the body of
the Mother, looking up into ropy yards of purple intestines;
rounded, red wombs; and thick, pink lungs.

Brushing aside the prickling bushes and thin tree limbs,
Kate had pointed to a series of small, ocher-colored handprints pressed against the bloodred stone. They were old
prints—older than any relatives I could ever hope to remember, as old as the rock itself. In hushed silence I stretched
high and fitted my hands atop the prints. Underneath my
palms the tiny brown fingers reached upward, barely touching the first joints of my own hands, which suddenly seemed
heavy-knuckled and ungainly.

The delicate brown hands belonged to "the ancestors,"
the first known inhabitants of the Eden-like valley the Mor-
mons later named Angel Canyon. Symbols they carved into
stone and their handprints pressed firmly against the rock
overhangs were like quiet voices reaching out hundreds of
years—perhaps as much as a thousand—across time. Under
my hands the red stone felt gritty and cool. I wondered
about the look and feel of the day these prints were made
and about the life of the one who had made them. The enduring mystery of the small prints tingled in my palms long
after I'd left the canyon.

Now, a year later, I was eager to share the wonder of
those prints with my husband. The trail to the prints was
no more than a foot's length wide, blanketed in red dirt
as fine and as soft as baby powder. As Lee and I walked, we
searched the path for rattlesnakes, which are common
throughout the canyon.

I slowed at a fork in the trail to get my bearings, and a
crow suddenly swooped low over my head. Startled, I
stopped in my tracks as the bird called out three times—*caw,*

caw, caw—and circled our heads. *Watch out!* Its wings were so close, they fanned my face, and I could hear the sound of feathers rustling like straw. I thought about rattlesnakes. The crow wheeled away. I looked at my feet. The path was clear, but my heart was pounding.

We pushed forward through the yucca and the swirls of red dust as I followed my memory. Curve left. Up around this boulder. Now behind the shrub wall. Yes, there's the tree! Stepping excitedly into the familiar, shaded clearing, I pointed upward. Lee followed the line of my finger. "Where?" He sounded confused.

My gaze followed his. The wall was bare. I blinked and stared, last year's vision superimposed upon the present. It was the right place. The exact place. But no matter how far we ranged from one stretch of wall to the other, there were no prints. "Maybe the rain washed them away . . . ," I offered lamely.

"After a thousand years? I don't think so," Lee countered. Once again I scanned the rock face. Nothing. Lee moved along the wall away from me, searching. "You're sure it was here?" He did not sound convinced. I followed him, noticing the knot of confusion in my stomach and ignoring the sensation of hair prickling up the back of my neck.

Our seeking took us around the cliff wall under a canopy of trees, into another shaded glen. Beneath a small rock overhang, a stretch of soft, vanilla-colored sand lay in waterlike patterns. The protrusion of stone itself stretched about four feet tall and curved into a perfect half-moon, forming a miniature amphitheater. Aimlessly I wandered toward it, my mind on the mysterious handprints. On top of the jutting rock was a chaotic pile of sticks, bottle caps, rusted tin pieces, and decayed leaves: an old, abandoned

pack-rat midden. My fingers began an absentminded exploration of its contents, turning over bits of old, charred
wood, sand-scrubbed glass, and small, painted triangles of
ancient pottery.

While I was still distracted, my eyes moved sightlessly
across my wandering fingers. Sections of the rubble began
to swim in and out of focus, as if viewed through a camera
lens fixed on a subject too close. Near my right hand, a
heaped mound of wood scraps shifted in my vision. Everything took on a dreamlike quality. Twigs. A pop-top cap.
Two small black-and-yellow beads, like cat's eyes. *Eyes.* Suddenly the heap reassembled itself with crystal clarity. The
undifferentiated mass focused and became three thick, mul-
ticolored rings. Black. Gray-green. Ivory. "Oh, God!" My
hand, a mere breath away from touching the sleek sides of a
coiled rattlesnake, leaped back to my chest, and I stumbled
backward in alarm.

"A rattlesnake! A rattlesnake, a rattle . . ." I could not
stop saying it over and over again. When I could find my
legs, I forced myself back toward the midden. The snake sat
stone-still, like an exquisite carving. Although I had never
seen a rattlesnake in the wild before, the moment seemed
unsettlingly familiar. Of course. How could I not recognize
this snake? He was the star of dozens, or maybe tens of
dozens, of past dreams in which I had watched my hand
reach into some dark crevice and encounter him. Each time
in the dreams, the sensation of breathlessness was upon
me. Was the snake poisonous? It was always my dream question. Now, looking at this very real snake on this very real
ledge, my question was answered.

The snake remained motionless. Although I knew my
safety was not an issue, I continued to shake. Lee asked me

why I was so agitated, and I could offer no answer. Leaning in close to the snake, I pulled my camera from around my neck and snapped off two quick pictures. Pulling out strands of my hair as an offering, I placed them beneath the midden. "Thank you for showing yourself to me in this way," I said quietly.

Lee and I headed back down the trail. We never found the handprints. When I questioned Kate later about their whereabouts, she looked at me curiously. "The handprints are on the other side of the canyon, over the river. There are no handprints along the trail we walked."

Weeks later back in Wyoming, I sat down at my dining room table with a cup of green herbal tea and an oatmeal cookie. Piled all around me were my collected books and papers on animal symbolism and mythology. I wrote in my journal, "Rattlesnake venom, although poisonous and deadly, is also used as a potent medicine. Rattlesnakes teach us how to turn something poisonous into something good."

Recalling my rattlesnake adventure rekindled the power that lies deep beneath a simple animal encounter, whether it be an actual animal in the wild, as was the snake, or an animal in the inner wild of dreams and visions. Evoking this power has nothing at all to do with the animal and everything to do with oneself. On a radio show one afternoon, a caller said to me, "I think you are granting animals a power far beyond their biological reality—which is their only real truth." Biological reality is the least interesting reality to me and has little to do with truth or with how I experience the wisdom of animals. That we are physical creatures sharing the world with other physical creatures is not what adds up to meaning in life.

Biological reality does not have arms big enough to hold the stuff of loyalty, devotion, integrity, strength of character, love, mystery. And it is these ideas, these strong threads of the absolute intangibles in life, that make up the multi-layered fabric of meaning. We meet animals in these numinous realms when we open our vision wide enough to surpass simple physical truth and bring our senses of wonder and possibility to the table.

Dismissing my rattlesnake encounter as a simple though surprising happenstance would render the experience without value for the challenges and changes that were facing me. In light of the fire, I felt that I was being asked by the spirit of a rattlesnake to consider my perception of poison and my perception of good, and how such things might relate to transition and homecoming. In my simple conscious mind, I do not think I would have awakened to the notion of poison's transforming into good. These ideas were born in partnership—my partnership not only with a snake but with an idea: an idea that animals, and we, are far more than our biological reality.

So much of my response to the calamity of my house fire was making itself evident in both sleeping and waking dream time that I felt I was being called by my soul not to ignore this precious landscape of insight. The world of insurance agents, of contractors, of bills, of simple and endless physical "doing," was not a place of peace or learning for me. It was a drain that sucked away my energies and added to my overall sense of smallness and exhaustion. Mystery and spiritual reverie were the forces providing comfort, healing, ideas, and hope. Mystery—the hardest force to prove, the hardest force to deny.

In pondering the message of the snake over many days and weeks, I began to realize that in the moments when I succumbed to tragic and fearful thinking—poison—I instantly transformed into my tiniest self. This smallest being of my psyche is wizened and shrunken, not from elderhood and wisdom but from fear. When she creeps over me, I feel her presence like a smothering blanket thrown over my head and tied with rawhide strings. I can't stretch my arms or straighten my neck, and I move in the world bent and afraid. Succumbing to fear created by my own thinking, I became far too small to face the task of maintaining any kind of a home, be it my inner home or a physical dwelling space.

As the days passed, I also began to see that tragic thinking was preventing me from feeling any connection with my Earth home. Feeling overwhelmed by the Earth in any way, we cannot feel as though we belong to her. Instead, we will guard ourselves from her and throw up defenses in thought and belief. But why would we feel afraid of the Earth?

In *Voice of the Earth*, by Theodore Roszak, I had read of an ominous theory by Sigmund Freud that spoke about a dark, devastating force of nature that Freud coined Thanatos, the death instinct.[1] Freud believed in his later years that the goal of all life is death. He viewed the wild as a place whose purpose was to kill life. "She destroys us," Freud wrote of nature, "coldly, cruelly, relentlessly." Existentialist Ernest Becker picked up the refrain from Freud: "Creation is a nightmare spectacular, taking place on a planet that has been soaked for hundreds of millions of years in the blood of all its creatures. . . . [T]he evil in the world is not only on the insides of people, but on the outside, in nature . . . [;] whatever man does on this planet has to be done in the lived truth of the terror of creation, of the grotesque, of the rumble of panic underneath everything."[2]

Roszak believes that the Thanatos theory is very much alive in psychotherapeutic history. It is a powerful idea that seems to have sunk deep into our cultural story, and I believe it is the reason so many of us feel—to put it simply— afraid in the woods. It is a fear I have felt many times, huddled in a sleeping bag in the middle of a moonless forest. Danger. Death. I recall the words to a childhood song: "The wood is full of shining eyes / the wood is full of creeping feet / the wood is full of tiny cries / you must not go to the wood at night!" How can I feel at home when annihilation is at my door, every minute of every day, when my Earth Mother wishes me destroyed? I spoke with a neighbor, a car manufacturer who lives at the edge of an aspen forest, about his feelings for wild nature. He answered honestly, "I don't feel that the wilderness has anything to do with the world I live in. The wild feels dangerous, because it is not part of my life. It's not part of me in any way, except for maybe some casual recreation."

As a child, I absorbed the cultural myth of the dangerous, dark wild as silently and invisibly as a plant absorbs nitrogen. I imagined monsters creeping into my windows at night from the scary blackness of my postage-stamp-sized suburban backyard. Night sounds frightened me, too. They seemed hushed and muted and secretive. I extended this fear to a virtual terror of insects. They were so very alien-looking to me, the stars of just about every horror film I'd ever seen except for *King Kong*. Bugs represented to me the fearful embodiment of everything I didn't understand about the world outside of my limited human confines. Spiders terrified me most of all. Always I seemed to find them in my bed, my "night place." And so spiders and darkness and wildness all became jumbled into a sinister sisterhood in my mind.

One night, when I was about nine years old, I was curled in my small twin bed reading something. I was always reading something. Out of the corner of my eye, I glimpsed a slight movement. Instantly I went stiff. A spider no bigger than a pea was making her tentative way across the endless expanse of my bedcovers. Her body was the color and size of a small pearl, her legs deep espresso brown. My face contorted at the sight of her, and I heard the shriek explode out of my lungs with the force of a whale spouting. By the time my mom arrived with a tissue and squashed her, I was close to hyperventilation. That night I left every light in my room burning and slept with the covers over my head and packed like a cement casing around me.

That something as harmless as an innocent spider coming to visit in the night should throw me into such paroxysms of fear, sleeplessness, and trembling speaks to me of the power of Freud's theory. I'm certain I was not born afraid of the dark or of spiders. In fact, I was conceived in darkness and lived there happily for nine cozy months. As a youngster, I had never been bitten by a spider. These fears and countless others I absorbed from the body of my culture. Our cultural myths about the foreignness, the danger, of wild nature and of her children—the rats, the bats, the spiders, the wasps, the wolves, the snakes, the dark, the storms, the silence—were old ones, well in place by the time the first settlers arrived in this country. I had even written about this fear of the wild Earth in my first book but had never realized how deeply a prisoner I was to it. "What is not useful is vicious," wrote Puritan leader Cotton Mather. I had never heard those words as a child, but somehow I had absorbed them. That is exactly how I felt about spiders, about the night. They were of no use *to me*, so they were vicious.

Decades later, having worked hard to conquer my fears of insects, I would read about the mythology of the spider and about Spider as creator of the first alphabet. I believe now that Spider was calling me to my true work and that my fear of Spider had much to do with my fears of claiming my dormant skills as a writer—as a weaver of alphabets. As with the rattlesnake who came to me, spiders taught me that something poisonous can be transformed into something good. The "something poisonous" in this case was not the spider herself but my terrible, debilitating fear of her.

It is not possible for me to feel at home in the world that my culture has envisioned for me. But the rattlesnake held tight to an image of poison transformed into medicine and offered that vision up to me, beckoning me to follow. Where in my own world had I seen poison and death transformed into good?

Twelve years before, cancer had tried valiantly to evict me from the home that was my body. I had fought cancer and named it poison, because it meant destruction to me. My battle, for a long time, was a dreadfully fearful one, with metaphoric darkness and wilderness lurking around every corner. It was not until I came to grudgingly accept that cancer was the most amazing and transforming event that had ever come into my life that my fears began to subside and my physical health began to return. In putting aside tragic thinking, in coming to view cancer as a strange sort of spiritual medicine, I grew from my shrunken self into a larger soul-body, a body big and strong enough to protect and reclaim my physical body.

I visited Yellowstone Park the spring after the blaze, following my radiation treatments. All around me I saw the remains of poison, of a flaming death that had claimed so much ground. Trees and bushes were burned into blackened spears, and all my footprints left smudges of soot wherever I walked. There is a stunning kind of silence in an area that has been burned, the silence of a breath held. It sounds like—but is not—the silence of a graveyard. That kind of silence is born of grief, shock, and remembrance of lives lost. The quiet of a burned forest is the hush of the world waiting for something, listening for something.

Perhaps Sigmund Freud had never had an opportunity to walk in a burned-out forest. Certainly he had never survived cancer. Walking through the soot of Yellowstone, remembering the destruction of my cancer journey, I understood that the goal of life, simply, *is life.* Death is no final goal but rather a tonic, a medicine, that fuels and feeds new life. Understanding this law of life is the alchemy that transforms poison into good and grants golden moments of strength and faith to the alchemist.

The magic that reached out to meet me in Yellowstone was in the incomparable mystery and power of tiny lives—of slender shoots of green and yellow grasses and of wildflowers the size and translucence of a fly's wing. Each life, in the great family of things, is a tiny thing, too. It is green with hope and iridescent with an energy as fragile as thin ice, yet strong as the neck of a buffalo bent low over new grass.

Remembering, reclaiming this, then, would be a piece of my homecoming. Feeling welcomed in the world required the reframing of old ideas about challenge and destruction. Life is constantly beseeching us to revisit what we label poi-

son, to see if we might accept the challenge to don our al-
chemists' robes and transform the so-called poison into
medicine. Carl Hammerschlag calls this transformation "seeing in the dark."

"I think I see, but I am blind. I have sight but no vision.
What is the difference between sight and vision? Vision is
the capacity to believe in what my heart sees, what others
can't see. . . . All around us are those who can see in the dark."[3]
When asked by an interviewer about the impact of his dis-
ability, cosmologist and astrophysicist Stephen Hawking—
whose ALS (amyotrophic lateral sclerosis) has left him
immobilized and speechless—replied through a computer-
generated voice, "You know, what I do is, I think. I spend my
life thinking. . . . It's what I like most. Look how fortunate I
am—I have my mind and nothing to distract me from doing
what I do best."[4] Hammerschlag believes that Hawking "sees
in the dark." Hawking has learned how to transform poison
into medicine. The Earth holds countless medicines in her
plants and trees; in the mysteries of her seasons, stars, and
tides; in the healing powers of her great and ample body.
She offers soul medicine to us in the form of animal relatives
and the gifts of wisdom and insight they bring. To the Earth,
burning is simply a richly set table for life. And life is Earth's
amazing, loving gift to me. I am life. If the world welcomes
life, then surely, she welcomes me.

Twelve years before the destruction of my house, feeling
the fresh, red scar on my neck where the cancer had been
cut away, I could only imagine what new life would spring
into me as my tragic thoughts about the poison of cancer
were slowly transmuted into a new, fresh adventure. Today I
can freely admit that cancer was the beginning of a new life
for me—deeper and richer than I could ever have imagined.

Fingering the scar again, a scar grown so old and familiar that it has become an almost treasured part of me, I could look at my house in ruins and say, with some small measure of conviction, "Poison into good."

"Are you going to want any changes?" my contractor asked me as his crew filled up Dumpster after Dumpster with fire debris. *Changes?* Treading weakly in the muddy waters of my sodden thoughts, my head barely able to break the surface, I had honestly never considered changes to the house. "We're rebuilding. It's a good time for you to think about getting things the way you'd really like them. Let me work with you on this." Bill smiled at me broadly. Compact, strong, and capable, Bill was the original builder of my house, having lived in it for six years before he sold it to us and moved to a larger property down the road. When the walls were torn down after the fire, he saw his old construction notes penciled on the two-by-fours and cried.

Standing with Bill in the early morning sunshine, I suddenly looked at my house in a whole new way. It was empty, with the skeleton of a new roof appearing slowly on top. The walls were stripped of Sheetrock, and I could see the very bones of the house in wood-ribbed nakedness. For weeks before my salt ceremony, I had harbored an unspeakable fear of this house. Every time I turned the corner on the highway to home, I imagined smoke billowing from its new, pine-scented rafters. Walking inside the house itself, I expected the ceiling to collapse on my head, the walls to crash down on top of me and crush me like a small, flailing bug. As with my unconscious fears about my Earth home, I held on to an image of my house as poison—something heartless and cruel that had tried to destroy me and my family, to gobble us up in sour-smelling, toxic smoke. It nearly got the cats. It could have got me. My salt ceremony had quieted many of my fears but left me with a free-floating sense of "Now what?"

In the amber morning light, the house stood harmless and inviting, and walking across the hollow-sounding plywood floors, I began to dream. I could choose to view this home of mine no longer as a vacant threat, but as an open and untouched canvas. Bill invited me to make it mine in color and form and feel. Mentally I started running lists of carpet colors through my mind, seeking something that would hide dog fur and cat hair balls. The wall in the living room had always stifled the light from the front porch. I'd take it down. The back porch was no longer in existence, but it had been too narrow to accommodate the dogs and me on a summer afternoon. I'd extend it. And why not a cat door in the wall to the garage, while I was at it? And tile that wouldn't show the splotches from water bowl dribbles? *Why not make it mine?*

"I know it's a hell of a way to get a remodel," Bill joked with me. But I was excited and reanimated at the wonderful opportunity that my own sludgelike thoughts had barred from my awareness. I laughed back at Bill. "But a damned thorough way to clean a garage, wouldn't you say?" In the air behind me, I could swear I heard the dry, papery buzz of a rattlesnake tail.

6

Giveaway

I am sent. I'm sent and I thank you all,
grasses in all your forms—fire in all your forms—
sparrows and rabbits and mosquitoes and
butterflies and salmon and rattlesnakes,
for sharing yourselves with me for this time,
and I'm bringing it all back, every last atom, paid in full,
and I appreciate the loan.
—Daniel Quinn, *The Story of B*

"Did you see what the roofers got done today?" I asked Lee over a dinner of canned soup. "The old shingles are off now."

"No. I don't drive past the house. I come home another way." He was bent over the soup bowl, and I had a flash image of Goldilocks and the Three Bears. Lee is a big man with reddish hair, a full beard, and a perpetual slouch. He has always reminded me of a grizzly bear—mostly peaceable, occasionally prone to growls and posturing. He moves slowly, decides things slowly. The house we had rented after the fire was not big, and with Lee in it, it looked considerably smaller. He has always been a man to fill a room.

Our rental house was two miles away from our home. I named it the Earwig Palace because of the enormous numbers of these creatures that inhabited the place. The first night there, when I had decided to relax my tensions away in the rickety whirlpool tub, a squadron of earwigs launched across the room, hurtling in every direction when I turned on the jets. The tub had not been used in a long time and had become home and nesting grounds for the slender, brown, pincered creatures. The volley of biting insects raining down upon me was in no way relaxing, and I never used the tub again.

Also sharing the living space with us and our dogs and cats was an army of mice, or something small-footed that skittered through the walls and nibbled on plasterboard all night long. "What do they live on all winter?" I asked Lee. "Earwigs," he replied. It became a joke between us, one of very few. Our days had become achingly somber. The distance to our house from the rental place was only a fraction of the distance that had crept between us. The fire had burned us down to our bones, and I awoke one morning in horror, suddenly knowing that the skeleton of our relationship was brittle and unsound. The bones had become weakened by neglect, grief, and lack of passion and were failing to hold us upright.

I would watch Lee in the evenings sometimes, stealing quick, secretive glances at him. Always his face was bland, like a whitewashed fence that conceals whatever life is going on behind it. We had quit touching each other, and I realized that the touching had actually stopped long before the fire. Only after the fire did I notice that it was gone, because I needed it most then.

We did not argue. There was not that much emotion left in us. We became silent instead. We tended to our grief by ourselves, Lee burying himself in computer games and work and me scurrying around shopping for replacement dishes, a freezer, and dog beds. I would flop into bed early, exhausted by filing reams of insurance paperwork and managing construction details. Lee would stay up until the early hours of the morning, slipping into bed quietly to curl up under his side of the down comforter. I would awaken in an instant when he came into the room but stay silent, wasting the opportunity to talk, to share something, anything.

The fire did not destroy us. Rather, it had illuminated us and found us standing empty, resentful, and apart from each other in its harsh light. By the time we decided to begin speaking to each other again, there were no words left except good-bye. In shock we took off our wedding rings, put them in a drawer, and Lee began the numbing task of looking for somewhere else to live. I would stay on and see the house rebuilt.

The morning after our decision to separate, I walked the dogs down the snowy road to our house. The air smelled cold and flat. By the time we arrived at the barn, the donkeys were honking on the hill, and Fashion was nickering to me from the pasture. In my chaotic world, the barn had remained my place of respite. Hay was still stored in the loft, mounds of droppings still collected in familiar corners, and the water trough still needed daily filling. In the barn I could pretend that life had not changed, pulling me along by the seat of my pants while I kicked and bellowed.

There were elk and deer tracks in the snow all around

the corral and the tiny, stencil-like prints of crows and magpies. I knew that a small herd of cow elk was coming regularly, but I never saw them. Sometimes I imagined that their
cookie-cutter tracks in the crisp snow were spirit tracks,
there to remind me that Elk was still protecting me, just as
the bull had promised in my shamanic journey.

That morning I told my old horse that we would be
alone from now on. I told the donkeys about how Lee and I
had grown apart and that there was no putting us back together again, and then I sat down in the corral and cried and
cried for intimate dreams lost or never attained. In the black
and empty galaxies behind my eyelids, I saw Lee's face, his
dark, sad eyes heavy-lidded with tears of regret and hurt. I
felt his hands holding mine—gentle hands with slender fingers that engulfed my own.

There comes a point in the hard times of life when you
have had enough, and I passed through that door that morning. *Enough! My house has been taken. Why does my marriage have
to be taken, too?!* How many more losses? My torso felt tight
and crushed inward upon itself, my muscles pine-hard. I
wrapped my arms around my middle, to keep what was left
of me from scattering like dry needles in the wind and blowing away. Transition often comes upon us with a domino effect, one change falling down upon another, upon another.
While we struggle to smother the flames of the first fire, it
sends off sparks that ignite a host of other blazes in a circle
around us.

I did not return early to the Earwig Palace that day. Instead, I brushed Fashion and the donkeys until hair lay in
piles around their feet like colored clouds. While Arrow and
Strongheart gobbled down frozen pieces of manure like

choice bites of See's Candies, I scrubbed the water tank, shoveled out the corral, and covered the barn in fresh sawdust, performing my barn rituals with a heavy mind.

Voices whispered to me. One was David's, and it said, "You are your choices. If you don't like what you see, choose again." My writer's voice said, "Intention is everything." I had written those words in books. As I sat, I fingered one of the elk prints in the snow, recalling a film I'd seen at an Earth Day festival in Jackson. Wolves had moved back into Yellowstone and Teton Park, and biologists were taking miles of video footage of the dance between the elk herds and the wolf packs. I had stopped at a booth that was running a particularly intense sequence of predation. A wolf—large, black, and panting—was chasing a cow elk through deep snow.

The graceful cow never faltered, not even when a second wolf joined the first, both leaping high and clinging to either side of her throat. Still she trotted on, more than two hundred pounds of wolf hanging from her neck like a macabre necklace. It hurt to watch, and it would hurt to turn away from her. I stared, transfixed at her power, her endurance, at the lack of panic in her eye—her still and quiet eye—and the pace she kept, the pace of a heart beating. Suddenly it was over. She sank down and died with a convulsive shiver. The film went black.

Where was my heart? With the rejoicing wolves or with the cow who had lost everything, had everything taken from her in those few brief moments?

In *The Seat of the Soul*, Gary Zukav writes, "Only when we see through eyes that lack reverence . . . does the feeding of one animal upon another appear to be a cruel system instead of one where species learn to give to each other, where there is a natural give and take and sharing of energies between kingdoms."[1] It would be impossible to know what that cow elk had felt, pulled down by the weight of life hanging around her neck, everything taken. *Not taken*, murmured an insistent inner voice, *given*. *Given*. I recalled the words of my friend Teresa Martino: "The universe twinkles around us, swirling with the power that eats suns whole and drools out the gases that in turn become stars again. The world teaches us but the truth is hard. If we fear to look we will never know. Coal was once forests. Diamonds were trees under pressure and heat, the volcano of Earth's heart. All life helps all life. Everyone sees the works as they are. If you see life as all things fighting, then you will fight. If you see life as everything helping each other, then that is how you will live. . . . I don't know how I learned of the giveaway. I must have heard it somewhere and it lodged in my soul."[2]

The elk knew she had been singled out the moment the wolves moved into the herd. They looked at her and she at them. Much is written about this dance—the life-death waltz between predator and prey. Native people say that the cow elk is not taken so much as she gives herself away. She gives herself not to death but to life. Her flesh becomes the flesh of the wolf or the coyote. Molecules of her blood and bones feed the grass, and so she becomes grass. Her soul becomes all the bigger as her one body becomes many bodies, many living beings, through the magic of her giveaway.

Carl Hammerschlag writes, "The old Indians say that if you give away something that's important to you, your life is renewed. It means that *you* have the things, the things don't have you. If you can't give away your possessions, they will destroy you."[3]

Back at the Earwig Palace, above my bed, rested the fanned-out wing of a great horned owl. It had become a symbol to me of the magic and truth of the giveaway, a symbol whose power I had forgotten in the aftermath of the fire. I remembered how the wing had come to me two years before, as I was making preparations to host a community sweat lodge ceremony at David's house.

I was not qualified to conduct the sweat lodge ceremony myself and needed to ask David if he would honor me by serving as the lodge chief. Such a request requires gifts. Tobacco is traditional, but I also wanted to give something that had meaning for me, to express how much I valued the opportunity to host the ceremony and valued David as a friend and teacher. In looking through my things, I kept stumbling across my one and only eagle feather. A wing feather from a young bald eagle, it had come to me on a river walk with Arrow and Strongheart and had become one of my most precious, secret treasures. For an entire day, I spent moments alternately wrapping the feather for David, then unwrapping it, putting it back in the drawer, and looking for something else to give that would be easier to part with.

In the end, with a mixed sigh of resignation and excitement, I wrapped the feather up in a red bandana and tied a bundle of tobacco on top of it. When I presented it to David with my request that he serve as my lodge chief, I felt a great surge of peace and joy course through me as the feather left my fingers. *So this is what comes from giving away what is precious and dear.* I was only half right. The giveaway is a circle, and it widens as it comes back around to us, magnifying the blessings to the giver. As I turned to leave David's house that evening, he called out, "Wait just a minute, Susan." Returning from his bedroom, he carried the full wing of an owl, spread out in a magnificent fan. "I found this brother along the road. Isn't owl part of your medicine?" For many years I had felt a very strong healing connection between myself and the spirit of Owl. David placed the fan of soft gray and tan feathers in my hands. "I think this is yours," he said.

Blinking back tears, I stroked the wing, which rested in my palm as silky and light as an angel's wing. The significance of the gift did not escape me for an instant. For the gift of my one cherished eagle feather, a dozen feathers had returned to me—feathers from my spirit bird. My gift had returned to me tenfold, like a tithe.

My marriage, my house were two of my greatest treasures. What would I make of these losses, which hung around my neck like a pair of clinging, hungry wolves, if I saw myself as giving these things away rather than their being taken from me? What if my house were my giveaway to the spirit of fire? What if cancer were my giveaway to a higher level of learning and healing? What if my marriage were my giveaway to mystery? What if I were able to transform the memory of everything in my life I felt had ever been taken from me into my giveaway? How would life look then? Would my soul expand like a giant breath to embrace all that had received my gifts, and would my life become larger?

My friend Daniel Quinn chooses a different word than *giveaway*. He proposes that we are "sent." Not taken, but sent on a glorious journey back to the arms of Creation. "To each of us is given its moment in the blaze, its spark to be surrendered to another when it's sent, so that the blaze may go on. None may deny its spark to the general blaze, and live forever—not any at all. . . . Each—each!—is sent to another someday. . . . My death is the life of another, and I will stand again in the windswept grasses and look through the eyes of a fox and take to the air with the eagle and run in the track of the deer."[1] Because one is sent, or gives away, others will live and flourish. When viewed this way, all of life becomes a portrait of generosity and sharing. All are giving. All are being sent on a grand journey in which life blossoms, then transforms into other life over and over again.

When humans in my culture die, we put the gift of our body in sealed boxes, locking ourselves in coffins to ensure that we will feed no one—not the ground, not a worm, not the grass. Even in death, our culture teaches us to be stingy and cheap. Despite so many of us dying, the shortage in organ donations means the death of many who could be saved by our giveaway. While we still live, we live stingy, denying the deer a rosebud or a garden flower, killing the ants who parade like a marching band to the crumbs on our counters. We curse when raccoons, skunks, and crows invade our trash, unwilling even to be generous with our garbage.

In the larger, reverent vision, we have more to give away to life than our physical stuff. Our experiences, too, can be held close to us with tight, fearful fists, or they can be given away in story to perhaps bring insight and wisdom to others. Always we are called to give our gifts with respect for the cleansing, devouring hunger of spirit, which seeks to forever transform us, always killing us to the old and birthing us to the new. Spirit is *something moving*, say the Lakota people: *taku skanskan*—something in movement, spiritual vitality.

The previous winter, magpies had brought me another subtle teaching on shifting my vision from taking to giving.

The dialogue—the relationship—that developed over time between the magpies and me was wordless and perhaps even more profound because of its silence.

The magpie family took up residence in my barn the first spring following my return to the Rockies. They arrived with raucous sound and color, lighting up the skies around the barn with a magnificent sky show. Large black-and-white birds with tails like long, ebony ribbons, they swooped and dived through the air like Orcas moving through the ocean. And that was how I came to view them—onyx-and-ivory Orca birds dancing in oceans of blue Wyoming sky, breaching, spinning, sounding. Few neighbors had anything good to say about magpies. "They'll steal your dog food." "Ever see magpies on a downed cow? They'll pick the eyes out while the animal is still alive." "Nasty, dirty birds—noisy robbers."

I could not see them with such a jaundiced eye, knowing them as well as I did. That May I watched in fascination as they built a twig nest a yard high and two feet wide in the barn rafters. It was an impressive castle, a log palace built by artists not squashed by the limits of formal architectural design. As they built, inserting twigs here and there, they cocked their soot-black heads side to side and talked in soft, muttering singsong voices that sounded almost human. Sometimes I would hear the mother bird chuckle to herself as she arranged twigs, then rearranged them again and again. When they were not building and singing, they were riding the donkeys around the yard and picking flies off their backs, swooping down on the cats, teasing the dogs into a chase, and bringing the overflowing bucket of their enormous joy to each day.

When the building of the twig palace was complete and

the barn floor littered with mounds of discarded sticks, they took to the nest and sat. For weeks I would look to the barn rafters and see the shadowy head of the female magpie looking down at me, her black eyes shining like comets. One morning I walked into the barn and heard tiny mewing sounds high up in the twig palace: *mweeee, mweeee, mweeeee!* Seven babies nestled together like a pile of hairless kittens in the dusky light of the rafters. One week later, when I went out to muck the corral, I found the sad, soiled body of one of the young, all mouth and long legs and pinfeathers. I set the dead fledgling by the pasture fence and watched a buff-colored fox with tail like a flag come and carry it away that evening. The magpies knew about the giveaway. To the fox, they had given life for life. To me, they had given their gift of joy and exaltation. I vowed that I would try to be as good and generous a neighbor to them as they had been to me.

When the babies leaped from the twig palace a few weeks later, I was waiting with open hands to carry them to the safety of a nearby aspen grove. As I carried the last baby to the sanctuary of the trees, the mother magpie dived at my head, straight and fierce, and pierced my forehead with her beak. I wore her mark like a badge of honor.

The magpie family continued to visit me all summer, even returning one evening to the barn and the twig palace to sing to me from the rafters while I fed the animals and filled the water tanks. How could anyone not be simply enchanted with these wonderful and beautiful birds?

That fall, after the snow cover came and stayed, Fashion punctured herself on a protruding spike in the far pasture. The wound rested like a wet, red mouth near the top of her tail and ran deeper than my thumb. After I had tended it daily with salve, penicillin, and herbal tinctures, there came a black day when I experienced for the first time the other face of the magpie. Busy indoors with house projects, I didn't bother to watch what was happening up at the barn each day. All I knew was that Fashion's injury, which was closed to a tiny pucker each morning, was a red, gaping hole by evening. I assumed it was because she liked to roll each day in the snow, tearing her wound open in the process.

Then one brilliant sunny morning while I was out shoveling mountains of fresh snow off the back deck, I saw a flock of magpies circle around Fashion like a school of hungry fish and land on her rump. In surprised horror I watched as one by one they hung head down off her tail and picked chunks of flesh out of the puncture wound on her behind. As fast as the ocean of snow would allow, I waded into the pasture, shouting at the birds, who circled up and away with annoyed cries of indignation at having their morning meal so rudely interrupted.

That afternoon I was on the phone with my vet asking what I could do to protect my horse from the magpies, whom my heart no longer recognized as relatives. The birds were taking from me, taking from my horse, and my posture became hard and petrified, my mind shut and fearful. In an instant of protective fervor, I had reframed the birds into vicious hordes. No one including my vet had any creative suggestions for me, so I improvised. With a Buck knife, I cut a patch out of an old T-shirt, made a white flag that hung off Fashion's broad butt, and secured it there with a thick line of superglue. The next morning the birds viewed my handiwork with frustration and loud, rasping cries. Breakfast was over. As long as I kept the flag in place, Fashion's wound continued to heal. If the T-shirt piece fell off, the birds were on her in an instant, and we were back to square one.

When the birds would get to a bare-butted Fashion before I did, I was livid almost to the point of tears. I begrudged them their meager meal and felt the victim of what I believed in my emotional stupor to be a planned assault. Meanwhile Fashion seemed to have no upset around her wound. She didn't care whether the birds took care of it or I did. While I plowed, crazed, across the snowfields to chase away the feeding multitudes, Fashion stood stock-still, ears pricked, offering her flesh with no complaint. Perhaps the beaks of the birds felt good and relieved a healing itch. I don't know. I only know that she was far more composed about the matter than I.

Fashion, magpies, and I continued our odd dance until spring. The wound had healed to a thin red line when I noticed one morning that my most recent superglue flag had pulled free. I fed Fashion and hurried off to the house to get more cloth and glue. My race against the devil birds was on. As providence would have it, the phone rang the moment I stepped in the door and kept ringing with important calls for the next three hours. From my window I could see the magpies swirling around Fashion. By the time I got to the barn, it was past noon. I led Fashion into the barn and slid my hand down her hip, fully expecting to find the thin scar line transformed into a bloody, wet sore, but it remained clean and dry. The magpies had not touched her.

Clarity came in an instant, pulsing in on a tidal wave of humility that washed over me and weakened my knees. It was spring, and the ground was clearing in many places. Worms, seeds, the remains of old dog food, old grain, and winter-killed voles spread across the wet ground in an abundant buffet. The birds had taken from Fashion—had received from her—out of their winter need, and she had given away without protest. In a landscape covered with snow and ice, the few meager morsels of scab and blood from a willing horse must have been a godsend. The birds received Fashion's gift. She could have denied them with kicks and tail-flips, but she did not. And so they were sustained in this small way through the dark, killing months. On Fashion's back were the wet prints of birds ranging from her ears to her tail. It was spring, and instead of flesh, Fashion was now donating tufts of loose, dead winter hair for nesting material.

I took my cloth and glue back to the house, knowing that the magpies would not touch my horse again, and they didn't. Instead, they returned to the twig palace with their songs and their joy. Their feet and claws tickled the backs of the horses and donkeys like acupuncture needles, and the mewing, kittenlike sounds of four fledglings filled the loft. The magpies danced and leaped in the deep blue sea of the sky, and gave and gave, and took graciously only what was given to them.

My afternoon at the barn was growing old. I thought of my beautiful bull elk who had been run off by snowmobiles a few weeks before because my neighbors would not give away, leaving a space as barren as a wind tunnel through my heart. I had been just as tight-hearted as my neighbors in my dialogue with the magpies. Life was asking me to become as generous as an old horse and to remember that the taste of giving, and of being sent into the great wonder, is a sweet taste that nourishes the soul.

My marriage would not be restored or rebuilt. Instead, I would offer it up as my giveaway to mystery and leave my hands up and open, not only in supplication and in longing but in trust. Where would my gift take root? In the deep cradle of insight and learning? In lessons of loss and grief? In a new way of seeing myself alone in the world? When I chose again, chose not only the circumstance but more important my holding of it and my naming of it, the bitterness released me. My muscles relaxed and went soft, and my tears were not burning acid on my cheeks but tiny drops of water. Generosity is a sacred tool to help us make meaning out of change and upheaval. In the giving we take our attention off ourselves and place it lovingly on another, putting to rest for a moment the overfocus on self that is a natural obstacle of transition.

I did know the heart of the elk who fell to the wolves. But I chose to imagine that it beat as a prayer of giveaway to the community of the living and that she ended her marriage to life with a splendid surge of longing, passion, and light.

That night I dreamed about Oregon in colors of lush green and loamy brown. I smelled rain on the air and touched the giant hemlock tree that stood outside my beloved Oregon farm. I dreamed of chickens on the clover lawns and llamas waltzing in the tiny pastures. Starlings sang from the mountain ash trees, which hung heavy with brilliant red berries. I dreamed of home.

Waking came hard. Even though nearly three years had passed, I had not been able to look at pictures of the farm I had left behind. It still hurt too much, like thick-edged rocks falling on my chest. I didn't know when I left Brightstar how much I would miss that home. I sold it lightly, thoughtlessly, and ran back to the Rockies, never giving consideration to how deeply lodged in my soul that small acre of Douglas firs and wild ferns had become.

Chin deep under the covers, I thought about a letter

from a reader of mine named Christine Davis. In it she told me about the death of her tiny dog, Martha, and how this death was the beginning of her writing journey. In tribute to Martha, Christine wrote the books *For Every Dog an Angel* and *For Every Cat an Angel*.[5] She wrote to me that Martha was her giveaway, the gift she had to give so that she could create the books that Martha, in dreams, instructed her to write.

I had written back to Christine:

> We have recently moved from Oregon to a new home in Wyoming—what I have always felt to be my soul's true home. I thought the move would be a dream come true, but it has been hard. Since coming to the Tetons, I have felt alone and misplaced. At the same time, I felt compelled to make this move. Each day I have asked myself, What have I done? I walk my dogs in the shadow of the Tetons while I grieve for the green of Oregon, for my old red barn, for my beloved trees. . . . This morning I read your letter and stopped short when I read the word *give-away*. I know that word, but I had forgotten it. As Martha was your giveaway, so my Oregon farm was mine. I, too, have needed to let something go so that there would be enough space in me for what is to come. When I miss my farm deeply, I will remember your wise words.

The missing continues, but I felt that morning deep within me a fuller honoring of the awesomeness of the farm giveaway. Brightstar Farm was my last memory of feeling "at home" in my life. The enormity of this giveaway cracked me open like a shattered vase to explore the notion of home-lessness. I would not—could not—have done this exploration living in the mothering arms of Brightstar in Oregon.

In the pewter light before dawn, I left my bed quietly so

as not to wake Lee, who moved restlessly on his side of the bed. We had both become sensitive, even in sleep, to keeping the center of the bed empty as a neutral zone. Soon, so very soon it frightened me, the bed would hold only me. I put on a heavy green jacket that encased me like a large pea pod and walked on crunching snow down the road to the home I had given away to fire. *I am sent*, I told myself. *I am sent*. The first bird of the morning called out in joy from the construction debris on the front porch. It was a clear, lovely sound, like a bell.

7

Refuge

*A group that doesn't take good care of its members
is a group that doesn't command much loyalty
(and probably won't last long).*
—Daniel Quinn, *Beyond Civilization*

On a frigid early evening in February, I found a loaf-sized package on my porch. It was a casserole, wrapped in a proud blanket of wrinkled tinfoil, made of the stuff of comfort—mushroom soup, egg noodles, string beans, and lots of melted cheese. It sat on the front steps of the Earwig Palace, waiting for me in the last rays of evening light when I returned with the dogs from feeding Fashion and the donkeys. Strongheart found it first and brought it to me with a sidestep dance of absolute delight. Thank heavens for the freezing weather, which had transformed the wonderful meal into a large ice cube. Otherwise, it would have been Strongheart's dinner instead of mine.

I did not know where it came from. For weeks such

11

things had been appearing anonymously on my porch. Foods of comfort and healing: chocolate chip cookies with lots of walnuts, gooey brownies as sticky as candy, a whole roasted stuffed chicken, soups loaded with cream and so thick a spoon would stand tall and upright in the bowl, unaided. I had no idea if they were the creations of one generous neighbor or of many.

I had always heard that catastrophe brings a community close but never experienced the miracle of this truth until the fire. When cancer struck me, I sought my healing alone. I decided on my path of treatment alone. I prayed alone. I cried alone. Most likely thinking that talking about my situation would just upset me, friends and family gave me the gift of their silence. I am a great believer in silence, but there are times when silence hurts rather than heals, and this was one of them. It was not until much later in my recovery process that I found my way into the extended family of cancer patients, which is almost a nation unto itself. In this community of common ground, I found courage, humor, and a real sense of belonging.

You might imagine that a house fire would be a lesser challenge than cancer. It must be easier on the human psyche to watch your house burn away than to watch your body wrestle to evict you. A house catastrophe is "out there," we imagine. Cancer is "in here." There is less difference between the two than you might think. The loss of a house and the loss of health are not so very different matters. Both signify enormous life changes. I have seen people recover from cancer, and I have since met people who have never recovered from a house fire. Both require that we rise fully to the challenge of the transitional journey.

One of the major differences between my experience of cancer and my experience of fire was that I was never alone in the reconstruction of my home. On the night of the blaze, one fireman joked to me that he never saw so many people living in one place. Evidently many neighbors walked down the driveway to the burning house and said, straight-faced, "I live here." These were the magic words that granted entrance. And so they came in droves. I had met only a few of them. But they came and they stayed until the fire burned out, offering me places to live, cars to drive, blankets to wrap around my mother, cardboard boxes to hold the remains of my office papers. Some brought flashlights; one brought bowls of dog food for Strongheart and Arrow. Rita, my nearest neighbor, brought hoses. All of them brought their tears and the shelter of their comforting embraces. I was never hugged so many times in one night in all my life.

The next day the neighbor men arrived with hammers and ladders and began tearing out the cabinets in the kitchen in a valiant but ultimately fruitless effort to save them. "Whatever you need," one elderly gentleman with pale blue eyes and a red hat said to me, "just you ask. We can get our hands on it."

I have lived in places where the community feeling was absent. Had my house burned there, I have a vision of neighbors roasting marshmallows and hot dogs over the burning timbers and taking video films in hopes of inclusion in some "real-life" television show. The warmth and genuine concern of my Wyoming neighbors touched me deeply. One memorable afternoon at the grocery store, a white-haired grandmother shared with me the story of her own house fire years ago. Animal companions had died, and all her belongings were lost, but she spoke with shining eyes and a warm smile and patted my hand and said, "Everything will be fine. You'll go on. You'll see."

Buoyed by the strength of strangers, I wondered how I could ever have survived that winter without them. In truth, I have lived much of my life outside the strong embrace of community. From my earliest years, I remember a sense of never quite fitting in anywhere. For years I thought there was something wrong with me. Then, in my teens, I decided that I was fine and there was something wrong with everybody else. As an adult, I swung back and forth between the two extremes. My family will tell you that I am the one who can be found curled up in a corner reading a magazine during a holiday gathering. My mother looks at me with mild rebuke as she tells me, "You aren't much into family."

I see myself on my back on my analyst's floral-printed couch. I am thirty-two years old, and Hal—a round, white-bearded Santa Claus of a man—is talking to me about my almost compulsive need to do everything myself. I tell him, "If I rely on anyone else for anything—money, companion-ship, help, whatever—I'll be in trouble if they leave. Like my parents—what if I accept their assistance in my life, and they die? They're getting on, you know. They'll be gone one of these days."

Hal leans back in his chair, clasping ham-sized hands behind his head. He lets out a long whistle, which ends with a rumbling chuckle. "Jeeez . . . ," he says, shaking his head. "OK, Susan, let me get this straight. So let's say I offer you a chocolate cake. And you say, 'No thanks, Hal, I've stopped eating cake because someday all the cakes may be gone, and then where will I be?' Have I got that right?" Yes, he had that right.

The house fire managed to burn away enough layers of my protective coating of independence to leave me exposed and singed. This time I would not come back into my house or into my jumbled life alone and under my own power. The flames compelled me to look closely at my concept of community and to explore what I had denied for so many years of my life—that we simply cannot live through change in a healthy way without it.

Intimate relationship is a small community. So is family. A community of friends is an intentional community of a sort. And then there is the larger community of neighbors, of races, of regions, of religions. We belong to many communities at once, but the tools we need to live successfully in community are universal, no matter whether we are speaking about the community of marriage or our larger relationship with all of Creation's community.

That my cancer had been a lonely battle had everything to say about me and little to say about the value of community. I was not ready to receive the gift of community at that time in my life, in part because I was not ready to give away—to share with the community the lessons cancer was bringing to me about healing. I was stingy and fearful, holding tight to my own experience, and so the world around me then looked stingy and fearful. But by the time the house fire hit, I had begun an opening process in my life: opening to sharing more of myself with the world and opening to gratitude. By the time of the fire, I was ready to listen again.

On the northeast end of the town of Jackson, a twenty-five-thousand–acre tract of hills, grassland, and marsh is home to the largest wintering community of elk on earth. Established in 1912, the Jackson Hole National Elk Refuge was created to provide a winter feeding ground for thousands of elk rendered homeless by the spread of ranch lands in and around the valley. After they were evicted from their ancestral feeding grounds, there came the bleak and terrible springs between 1909 and 1911 when the valley floor was carpeted with the dead bodies of thousands of winter-starved elk. They lay heaped in ragged piles around the bottoms of fenced-off haystacks, stretched like bleached deadwood in the stubble of hay fields. One old-timer claimed he could walk a mile across the valley floor on their skeletal bodies. An act of Congress created a winter feeding program, and from late fall until early spring, up to seventy-five hundred elk congregate like a thick hive on the refuge in easy view of the highway. It is an artificial setting ringed by wire-mesh fences, studded with metal Quonset huts, and crisscrossed with an angled web of rutted dirt roads. But the animals who winter there have made it a wild community.

When I returned to the Teton area to live, I passed the refuge often. Countless times I pulled over to park and just watch. I came to know the daily rhythms of the place and how the early morning hours would find the heavily antlered bulls resting in a congenial bachelor herd by the highway fence. I knew the places where the coyotes loved to hunt for voles under the snow and learned to quickly spot a winter kill by the cloud of ravens and magpies attending it. At the far north end of the refuge, the Teton buffalo herd roamed, taking some of the alfalfa pellets from the elk. The buffalo, even when far off and almost invisible to my binoculars, had a very characteristic shape, like huge meteorites nestled in the snow. At the refuge's south end, Flat Creek remained open and unfrozen for most of the winter and was awash in ducks and trumpeter swans.

Alone in my new community, I turned to the community of the refuge for company. Twice that winter I took horse-drawn sleigh rides into the midst of the elk herds and listened in fascination to the barking of cow elk, a sound so much like Arrow's woof that it was hard to believe it came out of the mouth of an elk. The refuge community was a living being unto itself, much like a man-of-war jellyfish, which is really not one animal but a cooperative conglomeration of tiny individual animals, gathering together for the good of the one and the good of the whole. It was a place of routine, of surprise, of giveaway, and of harmony in the truest sense. While the refuge was indeed a community, in the global sense the community was, in turn, a place of refuge.

From the elk that year I learned about the special community of the herd, a community in which there is truly comfort in numbers and individuality is of little consequence. Driving into town each day, leaving the elk behind me, I realized that my town trips were not simply the errand-running jaunts I claimed them to be. Like a herd animal, I was looking for the simple comfort of numbers. I found it in grocery stores, pressed against strangers in the tight lines of the checkout counter, and in tiny coffee shops that warmed me with the sound of earnest conversation rising into the air like steam over coffee cups. It didn't matter that my face was unknown. What mattered was the tender comfort of my kind.

Early the following winter, a local citizen turned down the Gros Ventre road toward home and watched a large,

husky-like dog cross the road in front of her car. It was limp-
ing, one paw held up and away from the snow. As she
slowed her car to look at the dog more closely, it sat down
on a snowbank, pointed its muzzle into the air, and sang out
a deep, plaintive howl. Wolves had arrived in Teton Park.

In my forays to the edge of the refuge that winter, I
learned about the community of a pack. In pack life, unlike a
herd, the individual matters. Packs are much smaller groups,
with strong leaders and formalized rules for behavior. Rituals for greeting, mating, hunting, and arguing bind the pack
community together, much as they do in human community. Ritual can help us make a collective transition sometimes, allowing us to confront, as a community, problems
and issues large enough to topple us as individuals.

That winter I also saw what happens when different living communities shake hands with one another. No matter
how much lip service we give to the wonder and delight of
diversity in our world, when it comes to living with it, we
too often fall short of our ideal. In my town many citizens
saw the coming of the wolves as more of a collision than a
handshake. More than a few complained that the wolves
would eat all of "our" elk. At town meetings about the
wolves, I heard muttering that we should "kill them all." One
woman wrote to the local paper of the horror of having
predators on a "refuge." She talked of elk having to run
helter-skelter for their lives and said that soon the children of the valley would be doing the same, as the wolves
turned their hunger upon helpless youngsters. Of course,
the wolves never came after the children. And I never saw
an elk run helter-skelter anywhere, except when chased by
humans on snowmobiles—an illegal practice that happens
nonetheless.

On February 20, just eight days before my forty-seventh birthday, a new member of the wild community showed up on the elk refuge to teach us all a powerful lesson in celebrating diversity, which we clearly needed. A mother cougar with three cubs chose a den high in the rocks of Miller Butte, within viewing distance of the main refuge road. Her visibility was unheard of. Intensely solitary by nature, the cougar strolled out each evening onto the bluff, seemingly oblivious to the clicking of hundreds of cameras and a loud cacophony of *ooohs* and *ahhhhs* welling up from the tangle of cars and crowds below. Wildlife photographers from all over the country came to photograph her, having never once managed to catch a glimpse of the elusive northern panther in the wild before.

Her willingness to be seen remained a mystery to many but not to me. I had long believed that when a wild animal is seen, it often chooses to be seen, and it may actually be seeking to bring its energy to a certain place, perhaps even to a certain person. Joanne Lauk writes about this phenomenon in the insect kingdom and proposes that when a mass of insects moves into a garden, it is trying to bring attention to soil that is out of balance.[1] Animal communicator Sharon Callahan believes that wild animals will risk their lives to bring balance—or spiritual energy—into a community. The cougar, I believed, was bringing her energy to the refuge, as were the wolves, to bring that community back into ancient balance and to remind us humans what celebrating differences really looks like.

Over the weeks that followed, the cougar added her more solitary dance to that of pack and herd on the refuge. She taught our town by living example that the world has room for all of us, no matter how different we look and live.

Elk and wolves and cougars had danced together for hundreds of thousands of years and knew how to respect and accommodate differences. Without the confining encumbrance of words, the members of the refuge family spoke together. The wolves asked each elk for its life with a look. And with a look, the elk either gave away or didn't. The cougar asked the wolves for their kills with a strong and insistent voice, with the swipe of a clawed hand, and with ears pinned like flat aspen leaves to her head. With hackles speaking louder than words, the wolves either said yes or no or later. The ravens asked for their place at the kills, fluttering down in a black rush of wings, saying, "Now, now?" Sometimes the ravens would dive in boldly and claim their meal. Then the whole ordered arrangement would tumble into a cosmic giggle of the unexpected. In all cases everyone kept on showing up in some form—alive or not—at the table of life. I saw much of this dance not firsthand but on films taken of the refuge, and yet the grace and dignity of the wild community revealed itself even across yards of crisp celluloid.

A true, sustaining community is a circle, a round dance of giving and receiving. So solid in their identity as wolf, cougar, raven, swan, elk, so assured of their place in the circular scheme of things, the refuge animals brought a deep sense of grounding to my life. I drew energy from them by simply watching them and breathing in their confidence and self-composure, hoping that somehow my respect and delight in them would touch them in some way and complete the circle between us of give and take. Lakota holy man Black Elk wrote many years ago, "The Power of the World always works in circles, and everything tries to be round. . . . Everything the Power of the World does is done in a circle. The sky is round, and I have heard that the Earth is round, like a ball, and so are all the stars. The wind, in its greatest power, whirls. Birds make their nests in circles, for theirs is the same religion as ours."[2] The power of the circle is the power of inclusion, of connection, and of belonging. No creature is left out. Ever.

The refuge community became part of my community as well. Intuitively I sensed that the refuge animals were family of a kind to me. We shared the same valley, the same seasons, the same moon and stars. We all needed to eat, breathe, feel safe, love our children, endure the rough times, and celebrate the joy of living. Watching the order and harmony on the refuge helped me to envision similar qualities coming into my own life. In my new community, I sought roots, routine, a sense of belonging to the whole. The animals of the refuge offered me an example to follow, a simple, pure example uncluttered by words or political posturing.

In my reflections at the side of the refuge, I felt for the first time that I was an active part of all that glorious diversity as much as any animal out there. I had known this truth intellectually for a long time, but there at the edge of the wild, I began feeling my connection to the larger community for the first time. In *A Cry Unheard*, a book detailing the tragic medical consequences of loneliness, Dr. James Lynch writes, "No 'body,' whether human or animal, can live in a healthy condition so long as it is living in physical isolation from the rest of the living world. To the contrary, healthy lives are those lived in harmony with the rest of creation, including harmony with one's fellow man. . . . People [must come] back into a life where they live in integral harmony *as part of and with the rest of the living world, rather than living 'apart from' Nature."*[3]

Human ecologist Paul Shepard has written, "Wild animals are not our friends. They are uncompromisingly not us nor mindful of us, just as they differ among themselves." Although I am a great fan of Shepard's writings, I disagree with him in this instance. My experience and the experiences of many others attest to sudden, surprising, and profound moments of exchange between humans and wild creatures in which each was clearly mindful of the other. Shepard himself even alludes to such experiences, writing of a pair of falcons who—with a piece of lichen—engaged him in a game of catch and toss.

From cancer I learned that the human community alone was not big enough to empower my healing. The rest of Creation needed to be included in a full healing quest. This is true of a quest for community as well. Especially in times of crisis, it seems that species boundaries can blur and we can reach across tragedy to embrace one another—hand, paw, feather, and fin—even if only for an instant.

Many years ago I was working for the Marin Humane Society when someone brought in a young adult hummingbird that had been caught by a cat. The tiny bird rested in a tissue-lined jewelry box that had never held anything as precious, brilliant, or dazzling as the cargo it held then. I lifted the bird into my hand and felt a wave of nausea wash over me at the sight of her injured wing. Broken into jagged pieces, it hung from the bird's shoulder like a crushed flower petal. There could be no rescue for this hummingbird. I held her sadly on my open palm and could not have been more surprised when the tiny bird dusted herself off like a chicken after a dirt bath, teetered up the hillside of my hand, and came to perch confidently on my index finger. She began a thorough preening that included the remains of her useless wing, unmindful of my startled face a mere four inches away. I walked carefully to the employee kitchen with the bird on my finger and mixed her up a quick sugar drink. I don't imagine she had ever seen an eyedropper before, but she eagerly reached her sliverlike beak to the dropper and drained it in an instant.

When I put my face closer to marvel at her, she met my gaze, eye for eye. Hers was the size of a grain of translucent black sand. Mine was blue and as large as her body. Her boldness astonished me. How could something this small, with potentially everything in the world to fear, be so courageous? I had handled probably hundreds of wild animals in distress and seen none as calm and trusting as this brave-heart hummingbird. On some level she must have proclaimed me "safe." And that was that.

She did not seek me out in her crisis, but neither did she run from me. We faced each other across the catastrophe of her brokenness and came together for a too-brief few moments of gentle, sacred exchange. I had few heroes in my life at that time, but she instantly became one of them. That I could not offer her life and recovery was devastating to me. Perhaps that is why I can still carry her jeweled green face and starlike eyes with me a full twenty-five years across time.

A reader sent me a story I've since lost, copied from a wildlife journal dating back to the 1940s. In it a couple from the Northeast recount a story about a wolf that had visited near their property for weeks, nursing what seemed to be a badly infected foot. They watched helplessly as the wolf grew thinner and weaker and the winter snows piled up higher and deadlier. They put out chunks of meat, trying to help in the only way they knew how. Then, late one night, they were startled by the sound of scratching at their cabin window.

Outside stood the wolf, looking in at them, his paw scraping the window pane. Opening the door, they found him dizzy, glassy-eyed, rocking on long, shaking legs. They didn't, they said, use their logical minds again for the rest of the evening. Instead, the young man stepped outside and carried the terminally sick wolf into the house and set it beside the woodstove on a soft blanket. He wrote that he believed the wolf had come for help and had knocked knowingly and desperately at their door. And on that night, he could not imagine turning the animal away. They covered the wolf with a quilt and gave him a bowl of water. Together they stayed—husband, wife, wolf—until early morning, when the wolf died quietly.

It was this story about the wolf that helped me to believe a fantastic tale told to me by a young biologist. She was working in Los Angeles, biking to and from a laboratory each day, when, early one evening, she saw a coyote trying to cross a busy intersection and get to the open space of a cemetery on the other side. The biologist could not believe she was seeing a coyote in L.A., much less one trying to make her way across four lanes of rush-hour traffic. The inevitable happened. The coyote was struck by several cars as she raced for the sanctuary of green lawns and trees, but still she kept running, and running—straight into the arms of the biologist, who had jumped from her bike and kneeled, waiting, on the cemetery side of the street. She told me that the coyote died looking into her eyes while the traffic raced on, not one car stopping.

To me these stories speak to the next level of community, which is true communion. Communion calls community into deeper and more spiritual sharing. Communion reaches into our inner world and infuses us with wonder and healing, while community brings the comforting casseroles, the routine and the ritual, and the promise that the world will right itself again after hard times.

Hummingbird, Wolf, and Coyote show us what can happen when our world of compassion and sharing blossoms beyond our self-imposed limitations of time, space, and species and becomes boundless. Ever since my cancer journey, I have turned to animals again and again for comfort and healing. That animals would turn to us validates for me once more and with greater conviction my belief in the circular orbit of community.

In my neighborhood lives a fox who spends time with a huge Saint Bernard. Early mornings the red guy appears at the doghouse of the Saint and barks a greeting. The lumbering dog emerges, makes a play bow, and the two are into it for the morning. The fox and the Saint weave together one more piece of the fabric of true community, which knows no discrimination, which truly celebrates diversity.

To be a part of these rare moments, to experience them or simply to leave an open place in the heart to absorb and delight in the truth of them, requires us to leave the voices of culture and science behind and go somewhere deep inside for a while. Animals, capable of putting any and all barriers to community aside and willing to do so, call me again and again to do the same.

In my determination to apply what I'd learned from animals about community, I decided in the autumn before my house fire to form a women's wisdom circle. It would be a place where we women could share the journey of our lives and where we could be truly heard and sustained. I wanted the circle to be a place that would honor the parts of our lives that were dying and, out of that death, the parts of our lives that were just being born. Because the wild community wisely embraces all species, our group would of course include animals, mostly my dogs and cats. Strongheart learned to attend the meetings with an especially relaxed attitude, often punctuating our comments by touching us with his paw.

It was important to me that we gather in a circle. So once a month we met—and continue to meet—in my living room, around a circle cast on the surface of a large powwow drum. I create the circle from whatever moves me that day. In the course of a year, it has appeared as a circle of stones, a circle of animal statues, a circle of evergreen boughs, a circle of lit candles. In form it is always the same, yet in the making it is always unique.

We always begin with a small ceremony of some kind—the passing of smudge, the reading of a short poem, a pipe ceremony, a song, a moment of silence. These small acts help to quiet our minds and bring us into what we call sacred space. From this space we listen more deeply, more honestly, more carefully. Here in our circle, the words we say count because they are heard by hearts and not just ears. In our circle we strive to hear one another in the way that we imagine that Earth hears us.

The following passage from Jamie Sam's *The Thirteen Original Clan Mothers* has given the women of my circle the most exquisite example of the manner in which we are heard and answered by our Earth Mother. The excerpt begins with

Snowflake speaking to the Clan Mother, Wisdom Keeper: "Mother, every one of the Children of Earth has feelings and dreams according to his or her place in the scheme and balance of nature. When combined, all of those dreams and feelings make up the needs of the Children of Earth. The snowflakes are the messengers of those needs because our bodies hold the patterns of each individual dream. When Grandfather Sun's warmth melts our bodies into the water, the feelings of the collected dreams are poured into the Earth Mother's soil, giving her the understanding of her children's deepest desires. . . . Each snowflake holds the web of life's lessons as it is woven by one of the Children of Earth."[1]

We seek in the small community we have created with our circle to listen as we believe the Earth listens to us and as all communities large and small are called to listen: with appreciation for our differences, with respect and compassion, and with an intrinsic understanding that each dream touches not only the dreamer but every member of the dreamer's community in ways we can never fully imagine.

Here is a story about the power of our women's community, gathered in a circle, listening. It is late October. Meredith, the daughter of my good friend Janet, has asked for a special meeting of the circle. The women show up at my door in late afternoon with plates of cookies, trays of cheese, and affectionate chatter. Autumn sun spills like a bucket of honey into the living room. I have made a harvest circle with clippings from my garden: stalks off the raspberry bushes, bunches of dried rose hips still on the vine, grasses with spent seed heads. I light a piece of wormwood— called sacred sage—gathered from my pasture. As we pass it around and fan ourselves with the pungent smoke, the chatter dies into stillness. Meredith looks at her mother, then turns to us. She is seventeen and beautiful. "I'm pregnant," she says, "and I wanted to call this gathering to ask for your insight and your wisdom. Some of you have had children. Some of you haven't. But I value what you have to tell me."

The ensuing conversation ebbs and flows for two hours. David's wife, Star—a self-confessed Tennessee hillbilly—sighs and says, "Well, sometimes life just ain't no fairy tale. Sometimes Cinderella gets knocked up." We all belly-laugh, and Meredith climbs up into Star's lap, where Star holds her as a flower holds the sun and tenderly pats her long, blond hair. I have never had children, and the conversation fills me with longing for paths not taken and with fear for the enormous responsibility facing this child who is like a daughter to me. The fears are mine, not hers—fears that, upon reflection as I speak out loud, frame just one small reason why I have remained childless: fear of doing it wrong, fear of being tied down, fear of my own selfishness.

Meredith's situation touches us each in turn and causes each of us to look inward while speaking honestly to her. We bring her nothing but ourselves, and it is enough. I hear not one word of rebuke or frustration—only offerings of support and love, and an enthusiastic desire to participate in whatever Meredith chooses.

Meredith chose to keep her baby, a beautiful son she named Spencer. I've never met a happier, more trusting baby, nor a baby with so large a community of "grandmothers." Our women's circle has the privilege of being part of Spencer's large extended family. I believe we became that

Refuge • 129

family on the day Meredith gathered us together to listen and speak from our hearts.

Parker Palmer, in a delightful book called *Let Your Life Speak*, reminds us that community does not create abundance, but rather, "community is abundance." Evidence of this surrounds me, whether it be the memory of a copper-colored mountain lion gazing at me from a rocky ledge or the welcome sight of a simple, unadorned casserole waiting on my steps. The Earth whispers to me, *"Mitaku Oyasin,"* reminding me that I need never feel alone again.

On an early morning in March, the ground was still covered with snow, but streams of snowmelt had begun to sing down some of the canyons. I carried a bucket of sunflower seeds to the bird feeders. Since the burning of the house, I had not missed a day of filling them. The pine siskins, the most common visitors to the feeders, sang an especially sweet and cheerful song that could brighten the most somber and dark morning. On that day I felt low and moved slowly, as through pancake syrup, taking the feeders down and dumping the spent husks on the snow. The birds waited patiently in the aspen trees, chittering loudly. When the feeders were full, I sank down on my knees, not ready to return to the Earwig Palace, not ready to do anything. Settling down with the grace of a sack of potatoes falling from a truck, I held the plastic bucket with the remaining sunflower seeds in my lap.

In the next instant, the borders of my community broke wide open.

One tiny, hesitant pine siskin fluttered like a breath before my face. Bravely she hovered in the air like a child's toy helicopter, choosing, choosing. To the last bird, the flock fell silent. Her small toes, as fragile and thin as earring wires, reached out to the edge of the seed bucket on my lap and clasped hold. Her wings pulled in against her body like an old woman adjusting her winter coat, and she peered up at me.

My face hung over her like a pale moon. I could count each tiny, brown-flecked feather and see the rapid-fire movement of her breathing, scarcely believing how close she was. Clearly she was no normal bird. Perhaps she was an emissary. The instant she landed, the entire flock began whirring over my head.

And then they were upon me. I felt their tiny toenails in my hair and heard the beating of hundreds of wings like a chorus of heartbeats. I gasped when they began landing on my hands, my knees, my arms. The combined fluttering of their wings carried so much force that my hair blew away from my cheeks as they danced around my face. I reached slowly into the bucket and pulled out handfuls of seeds, turning my palms up. Two birds began a territorial battle on my wrist, leaping up and down and batting each other with their wings. On my other hand, one hunkered down like a fledgling and began spinning this way and that, opening her tiny mouth wide and begging me or any-one to put a seed in it. I had to blink my eyes to keep the tips of wings from grazing them, the birds hovered that close. They ate, preened, napped, argued, all over me and on me.

Like a snowflake coming to rest on the ground with a soundless flutter, time stopped. I sat in a cloud of tiny brown birds, mesmerized, blessed, anointed as Saint Francis must have felt when the flocks descended upon him. The melting snow streams must have brought to my Earth Mother my dream of sadness, and so she sent a flock of her children to comfort and cheer me and to bring me a moment of refuge in the dark of winter. And I listened to them as the Earth has listened to me, and we touched each other under gray Wyoming skies—wing to fingertip.

8

Dream Master

The dream is the small hidden door in the deepest and most intimate
sanctum of the soul, which opens into that primeval cosmic night
that was the soul long before there was a conscious ego
and will be soul far beyond what a conscious ego could ever reach.
—Carl Jung

As the winter months of reconstruction rolled on, a different aspect of my life suddenly began bubbling to the surface, seeking my attention and reminding me that it, too, had been touched by the flames of change: I had a third book under contract, a book that had yet to be written. The skeleton of that book had been assembled on the morning of January 5, the day my house burned down.

More than any other aspect of my life, my work has taught me that there is a force beyond comprehension, helping us along the path of our dreams with loving, gentle hands. It was time for me to look at my work again through new eyes and to consider what work had to teach me about change and transition. As I sat down at my computer with a large mug of coffee and a piece of buttered toast to contemplate my third manuscript, I realized that my reflections on work would actually be a renewed exploration of dream mastering.

It has taken me nearly all of my life to understand that my real "job"—my true work—is to learn the art of manifesting dreams, not by doing but by being. My good friend Gael gave this process the name "dream mastering." Dream mastering asks us to seek deeply and fully the dream of the heart and to work in partnership with the soul toward the dream's fulfillment. We are not the ones who fulfill the dream or "make it happen." Another force—mystery, spirit, God, soul, whatever name you give it—takes the power of dreams and, like wind filling the sails, uses that power to chart the best course.

Mystery steers the dream ship, not me. I am merely a grateful, excited passenger on the voyage, calling down the wind and watching the horizon with expectant eyes. If this sounds too simple, too lah-lah—believe me, it is not. Dream mastering demands enormous faith in a power outside of us and a devout willingness to surrender our need to tightly control our lives. It insists that we put ego into hibernation and come to the dreaming circle in innocence, dressed only in the cloak of vulnerability and humbleness. To master dreams, we must also become fearless. These lessons have been slow in coming and indescribably powerful in their effect on my life. And to be honest, although I titled this chapter "Dream Master," that is my goal, not my current dwelling space. At best, I am a dream apprentice.

My dreams have been calling to me from the time I was born, and I have been calling back, following my dreams down a path far too lengthy and serendipitous for me to have plotted alone. Along the journey I've learned many of the secrets of how dreams are truly born. By dreams I am referring to those yearnings, joys, and quests whose fulfillment will lead us to greater levels of personal authenticity and wholeness. Our dreams are the purpose of our lives, revealing to us what we are here to be and to become.

There is another kind of dream, too, a mysterious and deep dream of the soul that comes to us as a need, an urge that seems to have no relevance in our lives whatsoever but will not leave us. Its fulfillment fills us with a body sense of release and relief, but only our souls know the ultimate meaning of these deep dreams. My childhood dream of living in the Tetons was such a dream. To this day I have no real understanding of its true significance in my life, or of why I was called here so strongly.

Some of our dreams may be about authentic work for ourselves, while others may be a call to express certain qualities out in the world. The dreams calling us to embody certain virtues are the hardest to identify, and readers who tell me they can't find their dreams are most often looking for those dreams in the world of "do," not of "be." My dreams were easily revealed to me at a young age because they were about things I was to do in my life. If my soul-call had been to express the quality of, say, gentle surrender to life, it would have taken me many years of maturing to identify that call, because it is a call that a child cannot compute.

My life began with three particular dreams: animals, writing, and speaking. I believe that we are each born with our dreams, carrying this magic down the birth canal in tight, baby fists. From my earliest days, my family described me as an "animal lover." That was my primary dream: *animal lover* was the phrase that defined me to my core, which is what dreams do. In the earliest photos taken of me, my chubby baby arms are full of animals: puppies, frogs, cats, chickens, caterpillars, moths—anything that moved. My identity as a girl who loved animals was the touchstone of my personal authenticity, to which I could return over and over again whenever I felt out of sync with myself. From infancy I wanted to be with animals.

My love of speaking was with me from the moment I learned to talk, believing as a toddler that people simply couldn't wait to hear what I had to say. I remember standing in front of our sofa before my parents' friends, waving my arms excitedly, telling stories about my day: about the bug I found, the peas my dad fed me for lunch, the picture I made with crayons. Speaking so fast that my words fell all over themselves, I was vitally alive and trembling with the joyful energy of putting my voice out into the larger world. Speaking decades later in front of groups of up to a thousand, I still feel exactly the same way.

I wrote my first book—the story of a shy, yellow dragon—when I was ten, reading it aloud to a squealing, applauding class of first-graders. I remember my seventh-grade teacher's reading a short-story assignment of mine to the class and telling me, "I don't believe this. This is really, *really* good." Writing was easy and fun. So was giving book reports—mostly books about animals—in front of the class. As a child, however, I never heard from anyone that what mattered to me, what lit me up from the inside out, was of any importance.

In high school there came a time when our counselors began asking us what we intended to be when we grew up.

Mr. Able called me into his office—one of those window-
less, musty-smelling places—and put the question to me.
"What do you intend to do after high school, Susan?"

"I want to be a veterinarian or maybe a biologist or a zo-
ologist, I think." These were the only animal-oriented ca-
reers I knew about. Mr. Able shuffled through what I suppose
were my high school test scores. Clearing his throat, he
leaned back in his chair and tossed the papers onto his desk
with a loud, final slap. "Your math and science skills are
really poor. Chemistry would kill you. Have you considered
maybe teaching? Your English grades are really good. Or
maybe you would like secretarial school?" That is what he
said. It was all that he said. What he *did not* say was, "Let's
look at this animal thing and see what else might be out
there. And has anyone ever told you that you are a really
good writer? I also see here that you've been really active in
drama and speech classes. What's that about?"

God protect our children from the tutor who is bored,
disinterested, tired, uncreative. God spare our children from
those who have never honored their own dreams. *English
teacher. Secretary.* The words hung like deflated balloons tied
in the stale air, and I squirmed in the stiff wooden chair.
There was nothing for me to say except, "I don't think so."
So for the next decade, I worked at any animal job I could
find: kennel cleaner, animal welfare worker, stable hand,
wildlife rehabilitator, vet assistant, zookeeper. Many of the
jobs were volunteer, and those for pay offered meager wages
at best.

Unbeknownst to me during this time, I was practicing two of the core tasks of dream mastering: holding
the dream in heart and in some way—any way—keeping the
dream energy alive in the world through activity. Kennel

cleaning and dog walking, while not glamorous, provided enough momentum in the right direction to keep my dream moving forward. It is a law of physics that it takes more energy to get a mass moving than it takes to steer that mass once it is up and rolling. I may not, in the eyes of my culture, have been moving very fast or in a particularly dynamic direction, but I was doing my part by feeding positive energy to my dream.

By the time I had reached my late twenties, however, the voice of my culture began to have its effect on me. Reflections of the world around me showed me tantalizing images of security, shiny new stuff, and social acceptance if I took charge of my life and got "a real job." Confused and torn, I ran away—far away. The man I was dating offered me the chance to explore the northwest coast and the Pacific Islands by boat, and I couldn't think of any reason not to go. Leaving family, friends, and work behind, I went sailing for two years on a yacht with billowing sails and sun-washed decks. At sea I was in every sense of the word adrift and without anchor. I felt the rising and falling of the waves announcing my utter lack of grounding to the soil of my life, and with it a deep fear arose inside me.

My sailboat—prophetically named *Spirit*—was offering me a unique opportunity to experience another necessary task of dream mastering: with the deep blue ocean beneath my feet rocking me up, down, and sideways for weeks on end, I was being given a profound lesson in the ultimate security of "not knowing." Learning to be at ease and relaxed in ever-shifting oceans of "don't know" is one of the greatest challenges in life. It is from this place of surrender to life that our dreams most easily steer us.

One night at sea, struggling with my fears of rootlessness, I was greeted by messengers who came to remind me of who I was. As *Spirit* sliced through the waters off Mexico, I stood under a night canopy of ice-brilliant stars, which fanned over the black water, horizon to horizon, sparkling like Christmas lights on the surface of the sea. The warm air was heavy with the taste of salt. I was on late watch at the helm, looking straight up at the mast as it bobbed from left to right with the ocean swells. Having become so used to the motion of the boat, I felt as though *Spirit* and I were standing still and the stars were weaving back and forth above our heads.

Far, far out on the sea's surface, I noticed a funny, murky spot of light under the water to the starboard side of the boat, like a flashlight beam shining up from deep under the water. It remained in one spot for a few moments, then suddenly turned and raced toward *Spirit* with alarming speed. My eyes opened wide in shock and fear, making out now two parallel lines of eerie green light speeding straight and fast as an arrow toward the side of the boat. A watcher of too many war movies, I imagined torpedoes barreling toward us, sent by some phantom submarine. Mere feet from the boat, the lines suddenly dived under the keel and quickly appeared on the port side, circling tightly, then exploding to the surface and into the air like a geyser of diamonds. Within that burst of light and color were the fluid, sleek bodies of two glorious dolphins. Up, up they went, like heavenly birds into the night sky, surrounded by a waterfall of pearly green-white phosphorescence that enveloped them in their own spotlight of dancing color and light. In unison they turned their noses to the water, pinned their fins like wings, and flew downward, hitting the water with a thunderous roar, spraying water into my face and splashing light up onto the deck. Again, they boiled to the surface, this time making *zweeet zweeeeet* sounds while they rolled and splashed in the wake of *Spirit*, calling out to me.

The light that was all around them seemed to come from within them, as though they were exuding the brilliance from their skins. I raced to the back of the boat and reached my hands over the water, my whole body alive with their joy. *Animal lover*—that was who I was, the dream energy lighting me up from inside like the phosphorescence beaming from the dolphins.

A hundred miles from shore, far from the siren call of a culture willing me to be something appropriate, something praiseworthy, the dolphins danced for me a joyous dance of simple authenticity. They danced who they were and what they were, on a rollicking, wet stage of "don't know"—don't know where the next fish is coming from, don't know what gift or surprise life might offer up in the next half hour. Two divine swimmers in the night that had no need to know, only to be. At that moment in my life, however, I lacked the maturity to absorb the dance of the dolphins and make it my own. I would need to fall even further away from my dream so that I could recognize it more clearly.

At port in La Paz, Mexico, I taxied with my boyfriend into town for a supply run. The day was blistering hot, the pavement burning my feet through my thin sandals. Outside the grocery store sat an emaciated, filthy orange kitten. Its eyes were cloudy, its nose caked in mucous. As people hurried by, the tiny creature struggled to stay out of the way of a sea of feet. A woman stepped on the kitten. A man kicked it out of the way, to the side of the door. Three children

blasted it gleefully with their squirt guns. The kitten stag-
gered, shaking its head side to side in confusion and pain.
Knocking shoppers out of the way, I ran over to the poor
animal and clutched her, a tiny female, to my chest. She was
so far gone that her body felt as light as air and as cold as
seawater. My boyfriend grabbed my arm. "Put that thing
down. You can't do it any good."

"I'll take her to the boat," I countered. "I can take care of
her. At least she won't suffer all alone."

"Put . . . it . . . *down*." His eyes were angry, his voice im-
patient and hard, and his words were not merely his own.
They were the words of my culture, telling me over and
over that dreams don't matter, that what was important to
me was meaningless and silly.

I hesitated, caught in the battleground of what I was and
what I was afraid to be. The sun beat down miserably while
the kitten nestled into my arms and nursed at my wrist with
small sucking noises. Reluctantly and with great shame, I set
the kitten down in a tiny spot of shade. She squeaked out a
weak, helpless meow, and I turned away in tears. In that instant I began to kill myself from the inside out.

After the kitten incident, I found myself increasingly at
moral odds with the others on my boat. My boyfriend had a
large family, and at one time or another, they all came in
groups to visit. *Spirit* would turn into a party cruiser at those
times, with everybody on board plundering the seas to the
maximum capacity of our one boat. Trash was thrown overboard; shoes were flung at birds stopping to roost at night
on our masts; a tiny bird who came to rest on the deck after
what must have been a grueling migratory journey was flung
overboard while I slept unknowing belowdecks. I was horrified and began complaining bitterly.

During a monthlong stay in the inland waters off Vancouver Island, family members fished, crabbed, clammed, and dove for abalone. Never mind legal limits—our guests observed none. I was horrified to see what was brought on deck: baby abalone the size of a tiny bar of soap, buckets of clams so numerous we could never hope to eat them all, a fifty-pound sack of sea bass, crabs heaped upon one another in traps stored on the back deck, where many would dry out and die before they could be eaten.

I registered my outrage about our needless waste of ocean lives and was informed that the guests would be served and that their right to a good time outweighed my moral indignation. My boyfriend told me this as he casually dumped a load of garbage off the side of the boat, along with a bucket of clams that had died for lack of oxygen. With a tight jaw, I answered, "Neptune won't forgive us this. We'll be made to pay."

One afternoon our visitors handed me a crab bucket up from the dinghy, and I looked in and saw a beautiful female Dungeness crab, her arms wrapped protectively around her belly, which fairly burst with the fat and glistening eggs stored there. I removed her gently from the bucket and placed her in a storage box on a pile of wet burlap sacks. Against the rags she shone purple and smooth. Her eyes on their slender stalks met mine, and I cringed in shame. Hers was the face of the sea, asking me why I had been such a willing party to all this desecration and disrespect. *Animal lover?* Surely that was someone else. It most certainly had not been me. That night, as crew and visitors played a noisy game of hearts, I slipped quietly away to the deck and under the light of the stars, returned the crab to the sea, along with buckets of clams and abalone, my tears and my apologies falling into the dark, clear waters with them.

Neptune *did* have his way with us. My sailing adventure was cut short when my boyfriend was suddenly, shockingly, diagnosed with cancer. He returned home for treatment, married his doctor, and died within a year. In my soul I know that my own cancer was born on *Spirit*. It would take years for the tumors to grow large enough to be discovered, but cancer's birth was there at sea, silently heralding the next stages of my dream. The sailing voyage became a turning point, a transitional journey of immense importance to me, although for years I would lament having gone to sea at all, believing the trip to be the most meaningless glitch in my already disjointed life. Throwing away old photographs, old writings of mine, old clothes, and old memories, I found I could not return to the life or the work I had left behind. Denying all the animal messengers who had come to me during my time at sea, I made a clear, conscious decision to put animal work behind me and seek out what my family and culture might call "a real job."

Because writing had been my second love, I settled on a career in technical editing. After taking extended editing courses through the local university, I landed my first position with an environmental engineering firm, working in the marketing department. My first paycheck was four times the size of anything I had ever made in my animal work. I wore a suit to work instead of overalls and had my own office and business cards. For the first time in my adult life, I had spending money, nice clothes, and a decent apartment.

It was also the first time in my adult life that I had no animal companion. I had put my animal dream aside.

The dream, however, would not put *me* aside. A dream is tenacious. It will always and endlessly send messengers, sometimes dressed as a friend or an interesting stranger, sometimes disguised in a gripping piece of writing or masked as coincidence or serendipity.

Sitting at my editing desk one afternoon, struggling against a deadline for a large proposal, I could swear I heard a cat meowing. I dismissed the sound until lunchtime, when I stepped outside and tilted my ears to the breeze. There it came again, far away, a dreamlike cry. Tracking the sound to a manhole cover in the middle of the parking lot, I lifted up the heavy, round grate. When I looked down, I saw a small tabby face peering up at me with wide, desperate eyes. This time, for reasons I cannot explain, I heard the call, loud as ocean waves crashing on the walls of my heart: *Will you remember us? Will you remember your dream?* Flinging aside my expensive red shoes, I crawled down into the storm sewer, shredding my stockings and soaking my wool suit in the process. I gently picked up the wet, feces-encrusted cat and wrapped her in my coat, remembering the terrible storm we'd had only ten days before. She must have been washed by the flooding rains into the sewer, then wandered imprisoned in the cold, dank underground for more than a week.

The employee cafeteria was only a few yards away, and I hurried there barefoot and filthy with my smelly bundle, quickly pulling a turkey sandwich out of the vending machine. Then I ran down the hall to the ladies room and rinsed off the cat while she scarfed down the sandwich— lettuce, mustard, onions, and all. For me the proposal work was over for the day, and my real work had begun. I checked out, citing a personal emergency, and left.

From the moment I picked her up in the sewer until I sat

with her less than an hour later at the emergency veterinarian's office, the sweet-faced, lovely young tabby never stopped purring. Her wet feet treaded gently on my lap, and she looked up at me with soft and trusting eyes. During her examination I told the veterinarian to spare no expense. I wanted her well, and I wanted her with me.

It was not to be. Her long ride in the storm sewer had damaged her internally, and she was in the final, terminal stages of peritonitis. The kindest thing we could offer was a painless death, and I held her close to me as the needle slid into her belly. Her lovely purr continued against my cheek until death silenced her. I left the veterinarian's office that afternoon emotionally shattered. The cat had cracked me wide open and then left me, her mission complete. She had called me back to my dream, and I would not forget it again. The following week I put a small aquarium on my desk at work and brought a conversational green parakeet home to my apartment. My editing work continued, but my remembrance of myself as an animal lover returned to prominence in my life, and I began seeking identity once more in that vision of myself.

Less than a year later, I was diagnosed with cancer. I thought then that the disease had come upon me because I had betrayed my dream for too long. Life is not so cruel. Cancer was another necessary piece of my true work, just as the editing work had been, although I could not yet see the full tapestry of my story in its fragments. With my first diagnosis, cancer reorganized the priorities in my life swiftly, completely, and eternally. My disease gave me a powerful incentive to make each moment count, as moments do when you truly understand that they are finite. Cancer also gave me another opportunity to find peace in "not knowing," sending me not into free float, as I had been on *Spirit*, but into free fall. This time I was ready for the lesson. The preciousness of life blossomed in my body, and with it the courage to return to my animal dreaming. With a prognosis of less than two years left to me, I made a promise to myself to live life as authentically and truthfully as my remaining time allowed. Risk taking became almost effortless. If I made mistakes along the way, so what? I did not expect to live long enough to suffer the consequences.

In the year following my initial cancer surgery, I wrote my first article about what animals teach us about healing. It sold quickly to a national dog magazine, and I was elated at the promise of seeing my writing published for the first time. But the invisible hand of mystery intervened, staying the publication date of my article for nearly two years. It was a hard lesson to learn: that the universe did not, and would not, work according to my timetable. It was in the span of those two years, however, that I first hatched the idea of writing a book about the wonder, the spirit, the healing magic of animals. I believe now that it was the idea that had traveled down the birth canal with me, waiting silently in my childless womb until I had matured enough to give it life. Two weeks before my article on animals and healing went to press, I called the magazine and told the editors that I was writing a book about animals and healing, and could they please add a tag line to the end of my article mentioning that I was looking for stories? They could and they did, and the mail has never stopped.

I had never written anything longer than a magazine article, and the idea of putting a book together was as terrifying to me as it was compelling. I had no clue where to begin, when Lee decided to throw a surprise birthday party for me.

One of the guests, a neighbor I had never met, was book publisher Maureen Michelsen of NewSage Press, who was deeply intrigued at the notion of a book about animals as teachers and healers. A week after my birthday party, she called me and said, "If you can come up with a manuscript I can work with, I'll publish it." I admitted to her that my enthusiasm far outweighed my ability, and miraculously she offered to steer me through the process. "Send me the chapters as you get them done. We can go from there."

Maureen was a gifted editor and teacher, and under her mentorship I learned how to craft a manuscript. Maureen's stepping into my life was an unforeseen miracle, something I could never have orchestrated by the sheer power of my own will. She had literally shown up at my door with all the skill, enthusiasm, and dedication needed to bring my dream to life.

Not until long after *Animals as Teachers and Healers* was completed and out in the world did I look back over the full journey of my work life and realize that every turn in the path had been engineered by some benevolent, wise, invisible hand toward the creation of that first book. The pieces and stories that never seemed to fit together took on a new meaning as I looked again, and from the vantage point of time, years, and intention, I could recognize the puzzle suddenly whole and seamless. My disjointed series of animal jobs had given me an enormous personal story bank. I could not have woven so many separate and unique stories together into a comfortable, easy-to-digest whole in my first book had it not been for years of editing experience, managing proposals that had been roughly assembled by many engineers with as many unique writing styles.

Looking back on my sailing adventure, I had learned

from the ocean that I was capable of functioning effectively through terror. Confronted by near-hurricane-force weather and seas sometimes thirty feet high, I held my own on watch and stood resolutely at the helm of my boat through black nights and screaming winds. I knew then that I would never be paralyzed by fear. Sometimes my book project washed over me in a black wave of self-criticism, inadequacy, and fears of failing, but because of my sailing experience, I knew that I could just keep going for as long as it took.

Cancer got my priorities in line, matured me to a great degree, and gave me the authority to speak on the subject of healing. The intensity of facing catastrophic illness filled me with an urgency and a zest that made my writing more alive and immediate. In the course of creating a book, all the parts of my life story reassembled themselves into such a new and well-organized look that many people—even people who knew me well enough to know better—imagined that I had planned it all. I had not. The dream held me in its hands from start to finish.

In living the dream, I have discovered still greater magic at work. I did not realize that the process is circular and that the dream had far greater gifts to offer me than I could ever hope to bring to it. Since putting my hand to the task of *Animals as Teachers and Healers*, I have discovered something truly amazing about dreams: *everything of importance in my life in the past seven years has come to me, or been revealed to me, through my work.* My books have brought me new friends, homes, opportunities, experiences. They have been another means of bringing myself into the circle of the giveaway: when we bring ourselves into alignment with our dream, the dream begins giving back, and it never stops.

My editor had told me to trust the process, the book process. But I found that the book process was teaching me something much more important: that I could trust my life, too. Powerful forces that I would never see and never fully understand were at work, calling me to believe in the wisdom of mystery. I had never planned to be a writer, an author, a speaker. I imagined as a child that I would best serve animals as a doctor or scientist. My life knew better. My part in the scheme of it all was to practice the art of the dream master, to put myself out into the swift current of my life and trust in this river of soul that carries us all.

In the hills above the Earwig Palace, a herd of deer grazed in the sagebrush. From my office in the back bedroom, I could see them like a school of tiny fish moving this way, then that way, across the snow. I pulled out my binoculars, and suddenly, as though given the cue, three of the does began to dance in the snow, tossing their heads down, then up, to some invisible winter melody. They bunched their delicate legs beneath them and, one after the other, leaped up high, bouncing like balls across the hill. Their dance looked joyous and frivolous, and I wondered why they would expend such precious winter energy in frolicking. The deer continued, though, springing past one another, bodies lithe, strong, sleek, like dolphins.

I remembered my ocean swimmers and their joyous dance of authenticity, letting the energy of their truest selves bubble up and over and out. The deer, too, knew the dance. Every animal does. It is a dance of joy and fearlessness, danced in deadly cold winters, in storming seas, and in the face of death and birth, danced to the humble, earthy rhythm of surrender.

In the time between jotting down my first book notes on

January 5 and returning to my book project months later, I discovered that I had come to another turning point within the greater turning point of my life that winter. Bent over my old notes and outlines from months before, I was stunned to find that I had outgrown them all. My proposed framework, my vision for the book—none of it held my attention anymore. Outside my window Arrow barked at a crow who had landed brazenly on her rawhide chew toy and begun pecking away. At my feet, rubbing her back luxuriously on my office carpet, Mirella purred and batted at my foot.

Life had diligently conspired to keep me from writing my book until after the fire, and suddenly I knew why. The book was to be *about* fire. Animals had steered me wisely and gently through my engagement with cancer. But cancer was thirteen years behind me. In the light of fire, what did animal wisdom have to say? What gifts did my wild animal neighbors offer me in relation to healing through crisis? And what had animals taught me about homecoming?

Fire touched my work with its brittle fingers, causing me to reevaluate, refine, and expand what I had been saying about the healing magic of animals since the publication of *Animals as Teachers and Healers.* Trust the process, I had been told, and so I brought out the photos of my burned house, pasted them above my computer, and began writing about fire while the deer frolicked outside.

House of My Belonging

O n the first of April, when the snowpack around the house was old and hard as an ice rink, I loaded up a truckful of belongings and moved back into my house. With the exception of my bedroom, all the rooms remained hollow shells, cluttered with construction dust and debris. I hung a shower curtain in the hallway and posted a SOMEONE LIVES BACK HERE NOW sign on it for the construction workers so they wouldn't tromp into my bedroom and bathroom without knocking. The bedroom heater didn't work, and the first time I used the shower, water spurted out of the wall. Still, I was home. That first night, the temperatures dipped into the teens, and outside my window stars hung like silver coins in the sky. Fashion stood silhouetted in the white

snowfields. Strongheart snored softly by the side of the bed,
Arrow by the foot, and the cats packed themselves alongside of me.

Except for the sounds of the animals, the house was
completely quiet, more so than I ever remembered it. The
day before, Lee had moved to a small room in a town house
forty miles away. The relationship to which I had belonged
was gone, and my spiritual sense of belonging to my life was
taxed by the energy required to keep my physical world
afloat. My house was in the place it had always been, and
the shape of it remained the same, yet it was not the home
I remembered. We had both changed and had become
strangers to each other.

In the still night hours, with the memory of the fire re-
ceding behind me, I rediscovered a deep need to belong
again to *something*. The uprootedness of my life after the fire
left me feeling disconnected, hollow as the empty rooms of
my house. Although a profound and sometimes extended
sense of disengagement is a normal part of any transition
journey, knowing that did not make me feel any better.
Celtic priest John O'Donohue writes, "To be human is to
belong. Belonging is a circle that embraces everything. . . .
The word 'belonging' holds together the two fundamental
aspects of life: Being and Longing, the longing of our Being
and the being of our Longing. . . . Our life's journey is the
task of refining our belonging so that it may become more
true, moving, good, and free."[1]

I was in need of a new sense of belonging in many areas
of my life. The house was a part of it all, I knew that, yet
there was more. "The longing to belong seems to be ancient
and is at the core of our nature," O'Donohue continues. "Belonging is deep; only in a superficial sense does it refer to

our external attachment to people, places, and things. It is
the living and passionate presence of the soul."[2]

In addition to feeling not at home in my house, I felt
again that I did not belong to the Earth—the sensation of
lost and apologetic anxiousness that had attended me since
my return to Wyoming. As the drama of the fire faded and I
returned to a home that felt nothing like home, I was hungry for tools that would secure within me a deep sense of
homecoming—to my house and to the rest of my world. In
Gaelic the word for *soul* means "the house of my belonging,"
and so I knew that the work of belonging, and the tasks that
attended it, would be soul work.

I fell into a fitful sleep, and in my dreams that night, I
traveled upon the sacred ground of my childhood. Braids
neatly ribboned, a bread-and-butter sandwich in hand, I navi-
gated the banks of a tiny creek that trickled through the
nearby hills just outside my industrial town of San Leandro,
California. My best girlfriend's father was an internist, and
Ann lived in a large, blue-roofed house on the banks of
that creek. In my dream I was bathed in the familiar, long-
forgotten glow of belonging to that time and place. Once
again I smelled the rich, leaf-mold muck of the creek bottom, watched the water bugs skate across its quiet surface,
and felt the succulent leaves of bay trees and willows brush
against my face as I pushed along the narrow corridor of the
stream bank.

When I awakened, the night was dwindling, and the
stars were beginning to wink out. I lay in bed, covers up to
my chin, and let the warm, sweet images of the dream melt
over me. San Leandro Creek had been a small patch of wild-
ish nature that drizzled from the spillway of a regional dam
and petered out at a huge culvert running under the streets

of town. At the edges of the culvert, gaunt men in too-big thrift-store coats slept away alcohol dreams to the sound of trickling water. Only once did Ann and I venture far enough downstream to stumble upon them, and we hurried away, quick-stepping over broken beer and wine bottles. Overcome by a dark, nameless fear, we never returned to that part of the creek again.

Upstream, though, was a different world altogether. Ann and I were captivated by the creek lands, one of the very few places in our town that wasn't taken over by gray sidewalks and squat little strip malls. After school we would hurry to her house, grab a sandwich or a handful of graham crackers, and slide down the weed-covered slope behind her house into the creek bed. We explored a two-mile stretch of that creek from the time we were in third grade until our young teen years overtook us with a kind of restless craziness that temporarily squashed out our longing for wet, muddy, web-infested tangles of wildness. By the time our longing for the wild returned, the San Leandro Creek was a distant childhood dream. I had followed the wild call to the Tetons, and Ann, to the tall mountains of Colorado.

Those years along the creek, however, remained precious in memory to us both. Perhaps because we were children and still steeped in the innocent glow of enchantment, we found ways of belonging to that creek that I had never quite recaptured in any place of my adulthood. I recalled timeless summer days sitting along its bank, listening to the drone of flies, caressed in sunlight that came down upon us in gentle golden dapples through the canopy of bay trees. As we sat, shoulders touching, we told a never-ending story to each other. It was a story that went on between us for several years, far sweeter than any we had read in books.

Speaking in confidential whispers, we imagined our-selves two inches tall and living in the wild tangle of the creek forest. In our fantasy lives, we sailed the creek water on leaf boats and tamed field mice to ride. Our make-believe house was a series of tiny caves that ran in a labyrinth inside the large boulder that sat in the center of the creek, dividing the water into two trickling tributaries probably only about a foot wide each. Bats became our airplanes and our friends, and we imagined tiny, soft beds for ourselves of dried grass and sponge moss. In our story we could be big or little, the creek granting us morphing powers. Within this fantasy ge-ography, the stories embraced the challenges in our lives, in-cluding boring teachers, bullying classmates, and our supreme lack of physical grace.

Our story world became a place for us to be as big in character and competency as we dreamed of being in our day-to-day lives. Under the filtered sunlight, toes making ripples in the warm water, we could feel strong, adept, beau-tiful, and loved as we sat nestled in the twin arms of story and place. When the silver shadows of late afternoon re-placed the dust-sparkled ladders of sunlight, we would stand up, brush off the grass and leaves stuck to our pleated skirts, put on our shoes, and walk quietly back to Ann's house.

Other houses sat along the creek, probably only twenty to fifty yards from its banks, yet to us, they seemed as far off as foreign countries. No one ever came from the houses to speak to us in all the years we ambled or sat along the banks. I think now of the book *The Mists of Avalon* and how the Isle of Avalon—the realm of the priestess and the Goddess—

could be neither seen nor entered by ordinary people. I
wonder now if Ann and I were perhaps children of Avalon,
unseen in the magical realms we conjured in that abused,
tired little creek.

Animals were not common there, heralding the losses
that would become worldwide in my adulthood. Now and
then I found a newt. Even less often, a frog. The animals we
most frequently found were dead: a large raccoon bloated
and ant-covered along our favorite trail; a doe broken to
pieces at the bottom of the spillway, most likely chased to
her demise by dogs; dead birds with their tiny eyes sunken
like spent seedpods.

Each death would necessitate a burial, and—except for
the doe, which was far larger than we were—we honored
them all with a carefully dug hole and a rock to mark the
grave. With our hands we would pat the mushroom-scented
dirt into a mound over the grave site and say prayers to ourselves, too self-conscious then to speak out loud of God. The
rock marker would be the biggest we could find and carry.
Sometimes we could only find a handful of small pebbles,
but we set them in place with great care. As children, we
more than understood the enormity of death: we felt it in
our bodies, and it was a heavy feeling that choked us into
whispers and made our limbs jerk and tremble.

One fall day after a tremendous rain and windstorm, we
found the creek clotted with fallen branches and mounded
leaves. The small flow of water had stopped, and the sub-
merging creek banks were black and boggy. Dressed in
plastic rain slickers, legs and hands scratched by sharp twigs
and broken tree limbs, we cleared away the mess, raking the
waterway clean with sticks and with our hands. When we

removed the last piles of soggy leaves mashed up against our boulder "home," the rush of free-flowing water exhilarated us no end and marked our new self-proclaimed status as creek stewards. From that day forward, we cleared trash and dead branches away from the waterside, and the grass grew up around the banks green and fresh. We tidied, we fussed, and with young hands wedded so closely to our hearts, we crafted a sense of home in that place—a sense of belonging so strong that I can still recall my feelings vividly, across forty years of time and distance. I can't say that, through my relationship with that creek, I loved all of Earth when I was ten years old, but I know I loved *that* earth, that small, tiny piece of it that was known so completely to me. C. L. Rawlins writes, "So maybe the earth is too big to love all at once, too great and various to be known by one work or image. . . . When I was four, I knew a horse. All horses, horsekind, the *Horse*, I have yet to know."[3]

Alongside my bed Arrow poked her nose against my hand, signaling her need to go outside. It was still predawn, when the sky is soft as an owl feather and the trees hold their breath. The spell of the dream clung to me, filling my entire body with a rich and sensuous tide of longing. The dream of my enchanted childhood place had evoked a priceless memory—a gift that would provide the tools I needed to bring that sense of homecoming into my current world.

Jungian psychologist Thomas Moore defines ecology as a search for home and belonging, writing of our need to belong to our Earth home as well as to our physical domicile. His writings were particularly valuable to me, as this was the kind of larger homecoming I was seeking. "Ecology," Moore writes, "is a sensibility, not a political position, and it requires profound education and initiation. . . . Deeper levels would include an attachment to place, ways of sustaining memory, and stories about places and objects that give them fantasy and therefore a basis for relationship."[4]

The creek of my childhood had become saturated with a soulful sense of home, or sacred ecology, in part by the fantasy stories Ann and I made up and shared together on its banks. Our stories honored the creek, our fascination with it, and our love for it. Through our stories the creek became not more than what it was but more *of* what it was—a tiny place of unspeakably precious earth and stone and water, with character and dignity of its own. And Ann and I became more of what we were, our stories highlighting the best of who we were and would become—courageous as we sailed our leaf boats, compassionate and intuitive young women capable of forming mysterious and tender partnerships with mice and bats.

Stories also gave Ann and me a way to be together in—and to create—sacred space. Sacred space is anywhere you are sitting that time and physical reality become suspended. It is a space that encourages reverie, daydreaming, introspection. It seems to have a special energy all its own. In sacred space the mind is invited to rest in its inner home. Ann and I created sacred space at the creek side over and over again, so that over time all we needed to do was walk toward the creek to be enveloped in a sense of the supernatural. The creek herself, I believe, responded to our presence and began to hold the sacred energy for us and our stories. Or perhaps the creek was the true storyteller, telling her fairy tale of communion with us in a voice we believed was ours.

The more we share stories in and about a place, the more precious that place becomes. Conversely, the more we take the time to explore and share the stories of our lives, the more precious we become to our own hearts. Storytelling is a way of belonging to ourselves, our place, our homes, and our lives. I thought about the stories I had told friends and neighbors about my house—how I came to find and buy it and how I nearly lost it. I had told stories of the barn and the magpies who lived in it and of the raspberry bushes in the garden, which produced glorious gallons of berries each summer. New stories had arisen as the house came back into herself, and I knew I needed to write and share those stories so that I could reconnect with the soul of my home, which had seemed lost to me for months.

When Moore writes of the value of relatedness in the task of sculpting a soul-sense of home, I am instantly aware that relatedness or relationship cannot exist without communication or exchange between us and the other. It really doesn't matter whether that "other" is a person, a dream, a rock, an animal, a tree, fire, air, whatever. Unless we are engaged together in some way, communicating *something* between us, there is no relationship and no sense of welcoming or homecoming. With our childhood fairy tales, Ann and I crafted an enduring exchange among the three of us: We gave the creek our time, our imagination, and our care. She, in turn, gave us back pieces of our souls and a deep sense of being welcomed.

Having had cancer lodge twice in my throat, communication is a theme in my life that I return to again and again, looking at it from different points of view, with different eyes. The topic never grows stale in me but always blossoms with new color and texture every time I approach it.

Communication in the context of finding a sense of belonging was yet another area of exploration for me.

I imagined that cancer had come to spur me into authentic communication, into the discovery and use of my
true voice in the world. In the months since the fire, however, I had been shown the other face of communication—
the role of the listener or receiver. The gifts of healing I had
been given over the winter were revealed to me because I
was listening for them. Speaking in true voice is a powerful
initiation into the world of the authentic self, but speaking is
only half the task, half the gift. Receiving is the other.

I had not defined this tool before as one of the marriage
partners of good communication, and just shifting my perception this way allowed me a whole new appreciation for
the art of the receiver, the listener. I had listened to dreams,
to ideas, to animals, and to landscapes as well as I knew
how. The thought arose in me, *How many other ways are there to
hear?* Were other voices speaking to me on a frequency I had
not yet learned to dial up? How do animals listen? How do
rocks listen? What do they listen *to?* Could those unheard
voices and unacknowledged sounds that seemed to keep the
world together help bring me into better relationship with
the mysteries of home and belonging?

The previous spring I had watched in amazement as the
Elk Refuge seemed to vacate overnight. One day six thousand elk were lounging in the melting snowfields; the next
day I could count only a handful. Who told them to leave?
No "chief elk" sets the migration agenda. So what is the
voice calling so strongly that it can lift six thousand animals
to their feet and set them in motion? One morning soon
after, I woke up before dawn and heard the hollow clattering

of hooves on river stone. Outside, a herd of maybe one hundred elk were on the move to spring pastures. Even in the deep gray of first dawn, I could see that they moved as though they were called to it, with heads up uncharacteristically high, feet tall-stepping, eyes intently fixed ahead. *We're coming.* That must have been what they were saying.

That fall I watched the annual migration of the Canadian geese out of the valley, hundreds of them flying in formation through the blue sky by day and across the pale face of the moon at night. Always, they called out in chorus, *guluuck, guluuck,* slicing through the high mountain air on silver-and-black wings. Like the elk, they appeared to have been called by some voice, their own harsh cry an answer to it.

Each spring mud daubers come to build intricate homes under my eaves. Poet Wendell Berry speculates that these insect beings may have a special way of speaking to the Earth to gain her cooperation: "Mud daubers . . . as they trowel mud into their nest's walls, hum to it, or at it, communicating a vibration that makes it easier to work, thus mastering their material by a kind of song."[5] I remember my Cherokee teacher David telling me that our voices were created so that we could talk and sing to Creator, our songs reaching spirit realms in a particularly effective way. Evidently mud daubers already know that. Perhaps all animals have such unique ways of speaking to the land that nurtures them, gaining cooperation and support through ways mysterious to us.

My dogs often awaken from a sound sleep suddenly to tip their heads and listen quizzically to nothing I can see or hear. I imagine that they are tuned in to some animal call just out of the range of my hearing, but my imaginings may be too limited. Who am I to say or to know that they are not listening to the Earth herself? Just the possibility of such voices calling delights me and soothes my restless spirit.

Author/naturalist Henry Beston describes animals as beings "gifted with extensions of the senses we have lost or never attained, living by voices we shall never hear."[6] How glorious it must be to hear the voice of the mother planet and how comforting. I want to learn how to hear those voices Beston claims we shall never hear. I believe I can if I listen not hard enough but tenderly enough.

In *The Voice of the Earth*, author and teacher Theodore Roszak explores chemist James Lovelock's Gaia hypothesis, the concept of the Earth as a living, self-regulating being. Writes Roszak, "Lovelock's hypothesis . . . held that all species in the planetary biomass act symbiotically to enhance the total life-giving potentiality of its planet. . . . [A]nd towards this end it transforms the planet into what might be viewed as a single self-regulating organism." Roszak muses over Gaia's intricate ability to speak to her "body" of creation, guiding all beings to ever-greater harmony and balance by means of instinct, chemical signals, and more and then goes on to ask, "How then does the great biospheric feedback system [Gaia] instruct and counsel us, its uniquely culture-bound, uniquely psychological species?"[7] He suggests that Gaia, our Earth Mother, speaks to us through our greatest tool, our minds. Perhaps, he suggests, the voices of the environmental advocates are actually the voice of Gaia speaking to these men, women, and children through dreams and mystery, asking them for help. Envisioning the Earth from this perspective, I may not be incorrect or sentimental in my belief that my childhood creek was perhaps the originator of my fairy tales, the voice of Gaia seeking ways to forge an enduring relationship through story with my friend and me.

One of the sounds or voices to which I have not given enough honor in my life is "the sound of peace," so named by my friend Maureen Fredrickson, a pioneer in the field of human-animal relationships and animal-assisted therapy. "A long time ago," she teaches,

> we lived with sounds that are, for the most part, lost to us now. Imagine the sound of a horse chewing grass. It is a sound that calls to us, and relaxes us. Now, imagine that sound magnified a hundred or a thousand times over. Imagine yourself sitting in a tiny shelter, fully surrounded by that sound. Imagine the night sounds of insects, soft wind and how it sounds as it moves through leaves and across acres of grass. This is how we used to live, im-mersed in these sounds of nature that were not blocked out with double-pane windows or drowned by the sounds of machinery. Could it be that over thousands of years, these nature sounds became embedded in us, a source of comfort, of quiet, of peace? Could it be that our hearts long for these lost conversations with wind across grass, water over stone, great herds bedding down for the night?

I remembered an afternoon I had spent out on Antelope Flats, close enough to the Teton Park buffalo herd to hear the sounds of grazing. For more than an hour, I sat—often with eyes closed in the protection of my car—listening to these sweet sounds of peace. I heard grass pulled and chewed, hooves on stone, sagebrush limbs collapsing as the buffalo lay down on them. The animals snorted and belched to one another and made deep, rumbling murmurs—almost like a purr—in their chests. Their breath blew out loudly in a dust-raising snuffle. These were sounds of such comfort that they lulled me into a drowsy afternoon nap.

Cardiologist James Lynch would agree with Fredrickson about the value in sounds of peace. He has made a life study of loneliness and its toxic effect on human health and concluded that we need heartfelt communication to be healthy, and even more, we need communion not only among humans: "Our approach essentially believes that no 'body,' whether human or animal, can live in a healthy condition so long as it is living in physical isolation from the rest of the living world."[8] Communication—sharing and receiving—is a profound component of our sense of belonging.

In my creek dream and subsequent reverie, I recalled how much of my relationship to that place had been forged with my bare hands. Following a hunch, I searched through my packed books for something I had read earlier that winter. Opening the pages of *Grandfather*, by Tom Brown Jr., I found what I was looking for: "Coyote then began to explain to Grandfather man's purpose on the earth. He said, 'Man is the tool of the Creator and Creation. Man can help nature do what would otherwise take many years. . . . As you see, the earth, this forest, once gave to me and I in return helped it to grow stronger. Man has an important part in the survival of creation, for it is through man that nature can grow strong and healthy.' . . . It is not enough to just care for the land when we are taking something from it, but to constantly work to help nature along."[9]

I closed the book, my heart saturated in the vision of a skinny little girl in braids, diligently clearing away leaves and sticks so that a trickle of a creek could flow. Clarissa Pinkola Estes, a Jungian psychologist and storyteller, includes storytelling and hand crafting in her clinical work as part of feeding the soul of her clients.[10] Finding my way to the house of my belonging, then, would involve putting my hands to the task of homecoming. As with dream mastering and finding true work, homecoming asks more than the involvement of mind alone. Homecoming needs the hands. Feeling welcomed by the Earth, our lives, our work, and our communities requires touching these things lovingly with our fingers and our actions.

When I had first moved back to Wyoming in the late fall, I had to wait until the winter snows unlocked their ice-grip on the land around my house before I could see and touch this new ground. That winter was a time of great disconnection for me, and I fell into the depths of depression before spring came and I could begin creating a sense of home by putting my hands on the land. When the days warmed and the sun burned away the winter, I walked around my Wyoming house picking up old branches and building a deadfall for small animals to burrow in. I broke apart old cow droppings with my hands, repaired fallen fence, and prepared a garden area with a shovel and an old hoe. These things I did almost instinctively, preferring not to wear gloves but to feel the dirt working into the creases of my hands and under my broken fingernails. "There is an extraordinary thing that takes place when you work the earth with your hands," writes Krishnamurti,[11] and while my mind was unaware of that truth, my hands seemed to know it well.

Every day that I put my hands in the dirt of my

property, I became more a relative to the place. "Attending to our experience, putting spirit back into our fingertips, allows us to redefine consciousness," writes David Suzuki. "Instead of being trapped inside, the mind becomes a reach, a region of care, the conversation we have with the garden around us."[12] Through the practice of the hands, I was unknowingly shifting my consciousness from "trespasser" to "relative."

The animals around me had their own ways of involving themselves intimately with their home lands. Arrow and Strongheart marked the perimeter of the property each day with hot streams of steaming yellow pee. Strongheart found favorite digging grounds, mounding up fresh dirt, which then became the gathering ground for every bird in the area. I watched a shy gray fox carefully lift his leg at each scentpost my dogs had so earnestly created, reminding us that this home ground was not ours alone.

Certain animals crossed the grounds regularly at night. I never saw them, but they left open trails through the grass and sage where wildflowers bloomed later in the summer. Moose nibbled on my raspberry bushes and trimmed back the willows, causing them to burst out with furious, thick new growth. I had read that each animal in the wild finds its special niche and immediately sets about bettering the place, to make it an even more beautiful, abundant home: "[L]iving things, once they appeared on the planet, took charge of the global environment in a creative way. They became full-fledged partners in the shaping of the Earth, its rocks and water and soil. . . . 'Living organisms have always, and actively, kept their planet fit for life.' "[13] The concept was part of Lovelock's Gaia principle.

The seed stashes of squirrels become new trees and

bushes in the spring; the vigorous pruning of the elk, deer, and moose stimulate new plant growth for more feed come summer. Birds sow seeds in their droppings; beavers engineer elaborate pond containers for the life-giving gift of water. Certainly this activity is in keeping with Tom Brown Jr.'s belief that our task here on Earth—as it is mirrored for us by all living beings—is to make this an even greater Eden.

I did not want my touch to be overly heavy on my land. I wanted to caress the land as my animal relatives were doing, not manhandle it. Over three years' time, I let much of the property return to tall grass and shrubs. Pulling out formal flowerbeds, I introduced native currant and serviceberry bushes to provide food and shelter for birds. Lawns became patches of wildflowers, which buzzed with the singing of insects and the high-pitched *whirr* of hummingbirds. The aspen trees near the house sprouted baby shoots all over, and I never cut down a single one, letting the carefully manicured groupings of original trees become an unruly, vibrant forest of saplings.

The soul of the pigtailed child still lived inside me, eager to tend, to beautify, to make room for more exuberant life. I would need to re-create my lost sense of home in the same way, waiting patiently for the snow to leave so that I could get outside with rakes and shovels and begin making a relative of the ground again. So much had changed in the course of the fire. So many bulldozers had run crisscross over the aspen seedlings and garden plot. It would be like starting all over again, but I had a good tool to begin with: my hands.

I sensed that feeling at home on Earth would require the same hands-on approach, and I vowed to keep the words of Tom Brown Jr. close to me whenever I walked in wildlands near and dear to me, like the lovely spring behind my house. Was there trash to be cleared away? A clogged stream? Some branches blocking the deer trails that I could pile up into a deadfall? What would it look like if I were to tie some colorful feathers onto the tree branches? Or stack some stones into a small monument near a grove of wildflowers, creating a natural altar space? Might simply honoring the beauty that was there with a small ceremony bring some good energy to the place? Guided by the child soul in me that delighted in fantasy, dreams, and imaginative play, I promised myself that I would seek creative ways to bring my own touch of beauty, in my own unique way, to the home lands I loved.

My dream of childhood enchantment and home offered me one more profoundly important piece in my search for belonging. Reflecting on the image of myself as a youngster in braids and denim pants, I knew the dream was asking me to consider the child and the gifts of the child. To find belonging, my dream suggested, we must return to our sense of childlike wonder, play, and—most important—innocence. "Innocence is not the prerogative of infants and puppies. . . . It is not lost to us," writes Annie Dillard. "It is there if you want it, free for the asking."[14] No matter what our age, innocence is a virtue required in the search for belonging. It is this sense of wonder, awe, and possibility that can marry us to home and place in a deep, reverent way.

"If I had influence with the good fairy who is supposed to preside over the christening of all children," writes Rachel Carson, "I should ask that her gift to each child in the world be a sense of wonder so indestructible that it would last throughout our life, as an unfailing antidote against bore-

dom and disenchantments of later years, the sterile preoccu-
pation with things that are artificial, the alienation from our
sources of strength."[15]

So much of the wonder of childhood comes from the
ability to play. Play opens us to joy, to creativity, to magic.
In ritual I feel most like a child at play. Like the games of
childhood, ritual is imbued with meaning far beyond the actual activities. In ritual, as in play, we transcend linear time
and flow into other realms of being. "Rituals," writes Margot
Adler, "have the power to reset the terms of the universe until we find ourselves suddenly and truly home."[16]

The previous winter I had watched a coyote hunt for
voles in a white, snow-swept pasture. She was a master,
pulling out a plump vole at every face-first dive she made
into the snow. Her hunting skill fascinated me, but what intrigued me even more was that between prey-stalking se-
quences, she would burst into fits of wild coyote abandon,
leaping high into the air, spinning in circles in the snow,
rolling feet up and waving to the sky. Winter is not a time
for levity in the wild, I believed, as energy must be carefully
conserved and spent. Yet how important must be the value
of play if a coyote would dance with joy in the cold, treach-
erous face of a high mountain winter?

By late May, as the construction workers were turning
their attention to the outside of the house, a hot and early
spring sent the raspberry bushes into full leaf. I poured myself a glass of sun tea, picked up a bucket of garden tools,
and headed out to prepare the bushes for summer. They
wanted trimming. The dead canes needed to be yanked out
and a trench dug between the rows to allow for regular flood
watering. The bushes had got away from me. As I cut the

twine off them, releasing them from the bundled clumps I created out of them each fall so that they could stand together under the weight of winter snows, they sprang out in a wild wall of shrubbery as tall as my head.

Carefully I worked my way between the two rows, crawling on my hands and knees down the tight corridor between them, to hand-trowel a small trench for watering. Leaves and twigs grabbed at my hair as I crept along, head down. My eyes were fixed on the dirt in front of me, and when I looked up for a moment to untangle my hair from a grasping branch, I fell into another world.

Above me the sunlight trickled sweetly between bright green leaves, which created a translucent umbrella over my head. From my seat on the ground, the cover of leaves looked a long way up, like a forest of thin green trees, holding hands with one another in the sky. *An enchanted forest,* I thought. *My enchanted raspberry forest.* Behind me I heard a rustling in the branches, and Mirella, my tabby, stepped into my magic world to stretch out on the warm earth. She looked over at me and blinked that lazy half-blink of contentment, and I half-blinked back at her. Around us the sounds of insects rose up in tiny, high-pitched voices. Old spiderwebs draped along the inside corridor like lace curtains, and the smell of the dirt was like warm bread.

Moving forward, I began humming a song as I turned the earth aside with my trowel. Mirella tracked beside me, grabbing at worms and grubs in the fresh dirt. I found two crow feathers among last year's brown leaves and tied them to the branches above me with a thread of leftover twine. They waved delicately in the thin breeze like silent wind chimes. A huge black beetle walked calmly ahead of us, shiny as obsidian, with antennae like slender shafts of grass.

I heard the construction trucks roll in and out of my driveway, but they sounded miles away. Workers were coming to lay tile in the kitchen and to stain the new cedar siding. I had offered to help them so that I could take an active part in the remaking of my house. Slowly, reluctantly, I turned around in the tight space and crawled back and out of the raspberry forest, leaving Mirella and the beetle to their wanderings. Overhead a hummingbird buzzed me so close I could hear its wings. Summer announced her coming on the breeze. On my way to the kitchen, I thought of the story I would tell my friends of the enchanted raspberry forest—a story of magic, delight, and belonging.

10

Leave-taking

*The heart has its own reasons. When we try to understand
why relationships come into being and fall apart . . .
we come face to face with the unknown core of the human heart. . . .
The heart is a mystery—not a puzzle that can't be solved,
but a mystery in the religious sense: unfathomable, beyond
manipulation, showing traces of the finger of God at work.*
—Thomas Moore, *Soul Mates*

"Stay away from moose right now," warned our local paper. "Cow moose are chasing off their yearling calves
as they prepare to birth their new spring babies." In the
process of separation, the mothers and their young get anxious, bad-tempered, and combative. Without warning they
will charge hikers and dogs, trampling violently with feet
like lances.

Home again in the sanctuary of my one finished room, I
realized that Lee and I had become like the moose. We were

trying to separate from nine years of marriage, and the feelings that fueled the distance we were trying to establish between us were unpleasant ones. When young animals leave the nest, they seldom leave willingly. The previous spring I had watched two magpie babies leap from their nest in my barn, heading off to the aspen groves with their parents in close, attentive pursuit. Two remained behind, watching quietly from the rafters, shifting their weight uncomfortably from foot to foot. The parent birds did not return. Still, the babies sat, vacant-eyed and quiet, gazing toward the barn floor almost twenty feet below them. For two days they remained in stunned silence, frozen in fear at the sudden turn their young lives had taken. Rarely did the parent birds return to feed them. Finally, on the third morning, I found them sitting together in the barn atop a bale of hay, their temporary paralysis behind them. Change had not come easy. It never does.

I had returned to the nest that Lee and I had forged together, but I returned alone. We carried different burdens as we struggled to make space between us. Because I was the one to instigate the separation, I bore the guilt of sending Lee out of our home. Lee, like the shock-faced magpie babies, had to step off into the complete unknown. I kept the animal family with me for comfort and company, a sense of secure routine, and because Lee could not possibly find a place to rent with dogs and cats. Lee had to go it alone in a strange town with no secure anchors of familiarity of place or people. The tension in our new arrangement set us at each other like a pair of angry raccoons. Blessedly there was no deep animosity between us, as there is with so many couples who divorce, yet the very dynamic of separating threw us into behaviors that were raw and desperate.

One evening Lee came by to visit Strongheart and
stepped for the first time back into the bedroom we had
shared, the room in which I was now living. My new desk—
the old one having been hosed to death—filled the corner
of the room that had once held Lee's dresser and books. The
carpet was a deep, lush green. Claiming the room as my
own, I had saturated it in the look of me, with animal drawings covering the walls, feathers and beads hanging from
lampshades and bookcases, stones and carvings atop every
surface. Plants sprouted in each corner, and a huge, golden
dragonfly kite hung from the ceiling fan. The space was
warm and lovely, and beautifully clean and fresh, with the
scent of new paint still clinging to the walls. Strongheart
and Arrow sprawled in the middle of the floor, their simple
presence adding to the sense of home. I saw Lee's entire
body sag as he stood in the center of the room. "This
is beautiful," he said quietly. I tensed up, feeling instantly
guilty for the good work I had done in carving out a piece of
home in an empty shell of a house. "My place is half the size
of this. A dump." I knew that his rented room was a jumble
of boxes and unfolded laundry, crammed full of stuff for
which there was no room. He looked at me with pain creas-
ing the corners of his eyes.

He wants something from me. Something, I told myself. *He thinks
I have no right to be here.* Pulling inside myself like a turtle under
siege, I lashed out hard to push him and his feelings away.

"This is no picnic," I fired back, glaring at him with a
look far harder than his comment had deserved. "The contractors are here every day, all day. The shower leaks, the
heater doesn't work. The insurance stuff never stops, and the
plow truck cost me nine hundred dollars to repair. You're
lucky the only responsibility you have is a room. Take this

place if you want it, and all the work that goes with it. You're welcome to it—all of it." I watched the pain drain from his eyes and anger flood in to replace it. I believed he was thinking that I always got what I wanted, that I always got the good stuff. It was an issue that had boiled between us for years. In turn, I was fuming over always having to do everything by myself, all the heavy and hard work. These kinds of projections that fuel themselves on words like *always* and *never* are an illusion, but between us they had come over time to feel as true as the hardness of rock.

Of course, I had no idea what Lee was really thinking, and my fantasy of always going it alone and doing all the heavy work was of my own making. In truth, he had been a helpful partner. The only beings in the room that night who had the good sense to be charitable and genuine were Arrow and Strongheart, who got up and wandered from one of us to the other with wagging tails and openhearted smiles, licking our hands with soft, sloppy kisses.

The feelings Lee and I struggled with over entitlement—about who owed what to whom and how we were going to get what we felt we were due—were horrible. They ate at me and left my face hard, haggard, and old. Inside my body greed and fear grabbed for control and left me achy and bent, and I stopped liking the woman I saw in the mirror each morning. Lee's despair was different from mine, but no less intense and self-destructive. It would be foolish and arrogant, even now, for me to speak for him and his pain. It is so easy, and so deadly, to presume another's feelings. I was left to intuit in the tone of his voice, his absence for days suddenly followed by a flood of phone calls, and the tears that often took him over when we were together, that he was in a hell of his own.

Weeks after he had moved out, he called and asked to meet me for lunch, with the pretense of discussing some practical issues about money and logistics. But when I arrived at the café, I saw that his face held more than small talk. With great courage he crossed the fragile bridge to me and offered his hand. "Susan, I'd let everything we have go if it came between our friendship. It isn't worth it." I stared into my bowl of chicken-chili soup, defenseless at last. That afternoon we promised each other that we would somehow find a way through the fearful attack garbage and craft a divorce that honored the time we had spent together and the friendship we dreamed of forging.

Regrettably we found few human models to follow. All around us were living stories of divorces from hell: stories of pain, deception, seething anger, revenge, and long-lived bitterness. We refused those stories. Instead, we each worked hard to become dream masters, holding the dream that we could remain friends. We also sat together in coffeehouses over steaming lattes and talked about turning poison into good, about what gifts we would find from letting each other out of the bonds of a poisonous, now-impossible marriage. We "looked again," as Carl Hammerschlag encouraged, and then again, and at each opportunity made conscious, difficult shifts in our perception and our vision of each other and marriage, seeking the ultimate meaning behind the story of our years together. Many days we fell short of our goals and sank into bitchiness and resentment, but always we came back to the table and looked again.

We remembered the value of ritual in nature and in our lives, and we sought our own. On a blustery spring day in May, Lee took his journal up to Signal Mountain, where we had listened together to the love call of the elk, and spent the day on his knees in tears, wailing out his sorrow over dreams lost or never attained between us. He wrote and prayed in that spot, which was sacred to us, and in his own way crafted a good-bye ceremony that was the beginning of his acceptance of our new path together as friends, not mates.

Around the same time, I attended a sweat lodge ceremony at David's place to welcome in the new growing season. I had growing of my own to do and decided to use the lodge to help me pull my heart back from my dying marriage and find the strength to craft a friendship instead. In the face of so much cultural pressure to just move on, to cut off anything and everything that had been between Lee and me, my quest took on the heroic intensity of a Greek myth. With a shiver I recalled the voice of my mother's boyfriend telling me, "People don't get divorced to be *friends*. They get divorced because they can't stand each other and can't stand to be *around* each other."

In the cool June afternoon, I prepared myself for the sweat lodge, called an *inipi* ceremony in the Sioux language. I had not eaten all day, choosing always to fast the day of a sweat. Donning a long skirt and long-sleeved shirt for the ceremony, I grabbed the tuna casserole out of my mother's oven and loaded up the car for my trip to David's house. Women dress very conservatively in the lodge, with long skirts or pants and modest tops. As David says, "This is a prayer ceremony, not a wet T-shirt contest." Always after the sweat, we have a community potluck meal to celebrate the ritual cleansing and purification that is the gift of the *inipi*.

David's lodge is large, holding up to thirty-five participants, and crafted of willow branches covered in tarps,

blankets, and plastic sheeting. When I arrived that afternoon, the fire was already blazing outside the lodge, and the
stones for the ceremony—twenty-nine in all—were red-
hot. I knew that earlier that day the stones had all been
blessed and prayed over. The fire had been built around
them and ignited with a burning stick on the east, south,
west, and north sides. The direction that flamed up most
vigorously would determine the primary energy for that particular sweat lodge: New Beginnings in the east quadrant,
Growth in the south, Introspection and Healing in the west,
and Wisdom and Death/Rebirth in the north. This fire, I was
told, had taken hold in the west. On the altar outside the
door of the sweat lodge rested David's medicine pipe, filled
with tobacco and ready to be smoked by all of us after the
sweat lodge ceremony was completed.

David called us all to gather at the lodge door at two in
the afternoon. Hawks had come to soar in lazy circles over
our heads. In all of the many lodges I have participated in at
David's, the hawks have always been in attendance. Filling
an old coffee can with hot coals, Teresa, the designated firekeeper for that day, sprinkled a handful of dried sage over
the embers and invited us each to bathe ourselves in the
cleansing smoke before we crawled on hands and knees into
the heart of the lodge. Inside, as a physical representation of
the womb of the Earth, the dim light of the lodge enveloped
me in a feeling of safety and maternal tenderness. Circling
around on my knees from the east-facing entrance of the
lodge heading clockwise, I stopped in the west and sat back
against the lodge poles and blankets. Behind me on the west
wall was the willow-framed, symbolic arch of the "spirit
door," the entrance point for spirits that would come to the
lodge to speak to us.

I sang quietly with the others as the lodge slowly filled up with two dozen from our loosely established "tribe" who had come for the ceremony, "Oh, Great Spirit / Earth, Sun, Sky, and Sea / You are inside and all around me." The lodge was a place I always felt welcomed and at home—a place for prayer unlike any I had ever experienced. The woody smell of the damp dirt and old cedar smoke, the tails of pray ties and feathers hanging from the ceiling, and the round dark-ness of the lodge itself—which would become utterly black when the door flap was closed—had come to comprise the most holy sanctuary I had ever known. Each sweat built upon the good history of the one preceding it, and so the lodge tradition had grown in meaning and value to me each time I had participated.

David called for a bucket of water and seven stones for the first prayer round. As the firekeeper passed the stones into the lodge to the accompaniment of drums and rattles, David carefully placed them with deer-antler tongs into the pit in the center of the lodge. He asked if I would please make an offering to each stone and handed me his bag of dried cedar, which I sprinkled sparingly with a prayer of thanks onto each stone as it arrived. "Thank you, grand-father stone, for your gifts and your wisdom. Thank you for sharing with the people," I whispered. The door closed then, dropping us into the dizzying world of complete black, and David began speaking as he ladled cold water on the seven rocks, which glowed with red faces in the pit. He re-minded us that we were in the womb of the Mother, that the gifts of rock, water, steam, and prayer would cleanse and pu-rify us. "You are cleansed of your garbage when you leave here. If you want to pick it back up on your way out and carry it along with you, that is your choice."

The first round of prayers and songs went quickly, with people offering prayers in intimate, confiding tones for new beginnings, for babies just come or coming, for new ideas, and for new leaves on trees tired from too many months of winter. The water sizzled on the rocks, and steam poured down on us, drenching our clothes and our faces. Sweat poured off of me, and I breathed in the wet steam with big, full gulps. After less than half an hour of prayers and singing, the door opened, the sun and the cool afternoon air rained in, and seven more rocks were slowly lowered into the pit.

I was waiting expectantly for the west round, the healing round, knowing that it was there that my prayers belonged. Traditionally it is the hottest round, the lodge having built up considerable heat after the previous two prayer rounds. When the door closed on the beginning of the third round, I scooted forward toward the edge of the firepit and, in the secrecy of the darkness, felt tears begin to course down my face. When David asked if there were any prayers, I quickly asked for permission to speak. Everyone in the lodge knew me and knew Lee. "Creator, Grandfather, Grandmother, I ask a blessing on my husband, Lee. Guide him through this difficult time of divorce. Hold him in your hands as he finds his new life. Thank you for our journey together and for the healing that comes when we learn to let go of what is not ours anymore." I said more, but what, I don't know. The steam was intense and insistent, pulling the energy out of my arms and legs. Sweat ran down my face, into my eyes and mouth, and I felt faint and sick. I murmured *"Aho,"* to signify that I was finished, and sagged back, propping myself up on weak arms.

The *inipi* brought no startling visions to me that day, no

lights bouncing in the black air as I had sometimes seen, nor visions in the eerie red light of the rocks. It brought, instead, comforting murmurs of sympathy from lodge members and a deep felt sense that I could, if I chose, leave much of the sorrow of my divorce behind me with the stones in the pit. More important, the ritual had acted as an emotional bowl or container from which I could more formally express my feelings and desires.

Crawling slowly from the lodge after the final, north round, I realized a soft stirring of lightness within myself, like bubbles rising from turbulent water. Bringing emotion and intent to the sweat ceremony had made it a powerful transitional ritual for me, and I was most grateful to find that some of the laughter that had left me months before found me again during dinner in David's cabin.

In the weeks to come, by focusing on transforming the poison of our divorce into something good, I found that spirits stepped in and acknowledged the earnestness of my dream for an enduring friendship with Lee by bringing me models of healthy separation in the lives of my animal relations.

Arrow, my collie and spiritual director, stayed close to my side—literally—during the weeks and months of early separation, reminding me through her relationship with Strongheart that friendship can endure a certain amount of bloodletting. When we had first brought Strongheart home as a five-month-old, clumsy, eighty-five-pound puppy, Arrow told me how delighted she was to have a dog friend of her own. Wiggling from nose to tail so vigorously that she nearly fell over, Arrow welcomed Strongheart into her home and heart instantly and with no reservations. What neither we nor Arrow realized in that first blush of new rela-

tionship was that befriending Strongheart was going to require extreme maturity, trust, and patience on Arrow's part.
Strongheart was a dog with a long and distinguished heritage of guardianship. A livestock-guarding dog from Turkey,
Strongheart was bred to claim and protect his property. As a
youngster, however, he was often misguided in the defini-
tion and execution of his life's work. Within a week of
Strongheart's arrival, he had commandeered the back porch,
the front half of the yard, the water bucket, and the driveway, claiming them for himself and denying Arrow access to
any of them. And he accomplished all this with what Lee
and I came to call "the look," a fixed side stare accompanied
by complete body stillness. It quickly became his trademark.
His level of self-assertiveness at such a tender age was flab-
bergasting to me.

Several times Arrow tried to gently explain to Strongheart that all these areas were hers also and that she was
very happy to share. Strongheart responded with growls,
lunges, and bared teeth. When Arrow came to me with puncture wounds in her back, we stepped in and took charge, letting Strongheart know that Arrow was his property, too,
and that claiming and protecting her were also his jobs. We
would growl at him and step in whenever he looked sideways at Arrow, so that he eventually learned that Arrow was
indeed his charge and his friend, not "the enemy."

Still, as Strongheart matured, he took his leadership
mantle seriously, forcing Arrow to defer to him in all dog
doings. She was to leave his food bowls and his toys alone.
If not monitored, he would claim her food bowl, bones, and
toys as well. If she stepped over some imaginary play line,
he would bite her and push her to the ground. At the same
time, his love for Arrow showed plainly on his broad, big

face. I had never before met a dog with such a deep range of expressiveness in his eyes, and those eyes clearly melted at the sight of Arrow, his beloved partner.

I watched all of this with mixed feelings. Often instinctively wanting to step in and overprotect Arrow, I forced myself to stop and look closely at the situation. In doing so, I saw that Arrow was actually deeply content with the arrangement, in every way letting me know that she adored Strongheart and treasured his friendship. Her eyes were happy, even when giving in to Strongheart's demands. Her energy remained high, her body posture alert and dancing with joy. Over the months and years, Arrow taught herself to accommodate, keeping a precise distance from Strongheart whenever he was eating, turning her head to the side and averting her eyes when she walked past him, and knowing just how far she could extend their play sessions. What mattered to her was his company and their deep affection for each other. She was willing to let a little blood fall at the outset to keep the relationship intact, giving new meaning to the old term *blood brothers*.

So many people asked me why I wanted to remain friends with my ex-husband when it was clearly so difficult to do in those early stages of divorce. Like Arrow's, my family is small, and because of that and more, I value friendship deeply. I had known Lee for nine years, and through the closeness of marriage, he had come to know me better than almost anyone. What is a friend if not someone who values you for who you are, warts and all? I was willing to let a little blood fall in the battles sometimes necessary to retain, reconstruct, and grow a lasting friendship. Sometimes with Lee I took on the role of Strongheart. Sometimes I was

Arrow. We traded off. Our bite marks healed, and they were worth the cost. Every time I see Arrow and Strongheart sitting side by side, elbows touching, I am reminded of that.

Strongheart had always been particularly close to Lee. In many ways they were alike—both of them very big, very bearlike in their slow, methodical approach to most activities. Both Lee and Strongheart were extremely sensitive and intuitive, and I worried when Lee moved out that Strongheart would plunge into depression, just as he had when we moved into the Earwig Palace. Their relationship would change again with Lee's coming and going, mostly to pick up and move his belongings.

Instead, Strongheart showed me that love and affection can remain even after the form of the relationship has changed. Greeting Lee at the gate with his characteristic toothy, ear-to-ear grin, Strongheart continued to adore Lee and to do something I often find impossible to do in my life—go with the flow. While I struggled with how to act around Lee now that we were friends instead of lovers, Strongheart simply followed his heart and offered the best of himself. He was pleased to see Lee when he could, affectionate as usual, and naturally disinclined to the resentments and hesitancies that are the result of overthinking anything. Slowly I overcame my self-consciousness at hugging Lee again, at smiling and joking with him. Remembering the best of who we were, a skill Strongheart always brought to a relationship, I was able to find the grounding for good dialogue between us, and it improved our budding friendship immeasurably.

Strongheart embodied another virtue that was to prove profoundly important in our separation and become its

greatest challenge as well. Self-composed, regal, and unas-
sailably comfortable in his skin, Strongheart has always been
our family icon of healthy boundaries. He is a kind dog, still
able in his adulthood to accept new animal and human
friends, but only within the limits he sets. Transgressing
those limits can be a frightening, unforgettable experience.
He has never liked anyone to lie on him or hug him around
the head and neck. He tolerates it from me, but only for a
brief amount of time. If I extend what he considers my invasive behavior, he will tell me so by moving and fidgeting. If I
continue, he will leap to his feet and roar—not bark but roar
like a lion—in my face.

I have warned friends about this, but one Thanksgiving
my friend Janet forgot, wandered over to where Strongheart
sprawled snoring on the rug, and lay down beside him with
her head on his shoulder. I was around the corner washing
dishes, when I heard an explosive roar that blasted through
the house. Running into the living room, I saw Janet on her
feet, white-faced, and Strongheart glaring at her. "I forgot,"
Janet sputtered. "He has his boundaries, and I forgot. I won't
forget again."

In trying to forge a friendship out of a divorce, I was far
less clear in my own boundaries, and my murkiness came
back to bite me again and again. I wanted distance from Lee,
yet I wanted our familiar closeness, too. I sent out mixed signals, sometimes calling on him for help, then pushing him
away with silence when I wanted alone time. There were
parts of us that I wanted to keep that cannot be kept in
friendship, and I was hesitant and afraid to let go. In the
confusion that I helped to create, Lee and I kept closer to
each other than was good for either of us. I remember my
unsettled feelings when I would not return his calls for a day

because I was gone or busy. He asked me once, "Where were you? What have you been doing?" I felt as if I were being asked to report in, and I resented it. Occasionally he would want to borrow things from me: my travel suitcase, a camp light, a hose. Always he was generous in offering his own belongings anytime I needed use of them, yet I felt as though his requests were like small ropes being knotted between, keeping us tied together, and I wanted to say, "No! Please, I can't share like when we were married!" Yet, unlike Strongheart, I could not roar or even fidget when I felt invaded. My inability to know and defend my boundaries was, and remains, one of the most difficult challenges between me and my former husband, and Strongheart remains my best teacher.

Outside of the relationship dynamics of the animals under my roof, I had watched the panorama of life change around me in my wild home, watching seasons shift with dramatic gestures of wind and color, noticing herds of elk and deer congregate on my hillside one year and abandon it the next, feeling the luxuriant green of summers when the water was abundant and the ache inside me during summers when the ground was as cracked dry and hard as old bone. Three times in the winter after the fire, I had sat hopefully at my bird feeder with my hands full of seeds, waiting for the pine siskins to alight on my arms and hands once again, but they never did. The time for that had come and gone, and life had moved on.

More than ever I noticed the ebb and flow of life in the wild world around me and saw how it related closely to the tides in each life, in my life. Native American healer Rolling Thunder speaks eloquently of the importance of timing: "There is a time and a place for everything. It's easy to say, but hard to understand. You have to live it to understand it."[1] Living in close proximity to a wild environment that seemed intrinsically, exquisitely bound to the dream of right time and place, I was beginning to absorb the truth of that natural law. There is a right time and place for everything that comes to us in our lives.

Our uncontested divorce moved through the courts swiftly, until the day came when my attorney called and said simply, "You're single again." For all the ceremony we had gone through to marry, to have our years together end on such a flat and meaningless note did not sit well with either of us. I suggested a good-bye ceremony, and Lee agreed. We drove to the top of Signal Mountain on a warm morning when the sky was cloudless. Carrying folding chairs, we hiked along the steep mountainside to a sheltered, secluded group of aspen trees that overlooked the valley below. I had brought my ceremonial pipe from David along, and as we began loading the pipe with tobacco, we offered prayers for each other and for the beautiful parts of life history that we shared, naming one by one the animal family members who had come and gone in our lives over the previous nine years.

We thanked Creator and each other for the good times and for the good qualities we saw and affirmed in each other. We cried and cried, and prayed again, and gave still more thanks. It was hours before we finally smoked the pipe, symbolically sending all of our prayers up in smoke to the ears of the Creator. In the grove of trees, we said farewell in a way that had meaning for us, and the ceremony left us feeling lighthearted and filled with hope and promise for our new beginnings by the time the last bit of tobacco was smoked away.

Walking back to the car, I thought again of the magpie

babies, those two who had stayed behind in shock and confusion, hunkering down in a deserted nest as Lee and I had
in the last year or two of our time as husband and wife.
Somehow we had found the courage to hear the call of right
timing that beckoned us to both an ending and a beginning,
and holding hands, we leaped.

11

Intimate
Nature

*At the heart and center of most fairy tales seem to lie crisis and a
conflict of balances between the masculine and the feminine, or the hero
and the heroine. . . . They meet, they part, they lose track of each
other, they suffer terrible fates. . . . How impossible that they should
ever meet, not to mention, remeet.*
—Gertrud Mueller Nelson

"Dear Susan, It has been several years since I wrote you
after reading *Animals as Teachers and Healers*. I enclosed
a picture of Mt. Moran reflected in the waters of Jackson
Lake, and you wrote back to me that you put it over your
desk. I have been through your spiritual land of wonder
many times recently, each trip wanting to meet you; however, I have missed you for one reason or another every
time. I will be there again in June. I would very much like to
meet you this time and perhaps have coffee with you.
Would this be possible? —Fritz Saam"

I recalled the soggy photo and the tiny handwritten

note attached to it on the floor of my office after the fire. Because of the volume of mail I get from readers, I seldom remember names, but I remembered this one. It was unusual, like the lovely photo that had graced my computer for three years before the house fire took it.

Reading the message on my computer, I felt uneasy. Readers had occasionally asked to meet me over the years, but they had always been women. Years before, I had changed to an unlisted phone number because of several calls—one at three in the morning—from men who had read my book, loved or hated it, and wanted to talk to me about it. The calls felt invasive and frightening. There was nothing confrontational about Fritz Saam's E-mail, but the simple fact that the request had come from a man set me to thinking about stalkers and ax murderers.

Lee and I had been apart for three months, and I had decided in that time that I clearly intended to remain single and alone for the rest of my life. A long string of poor relationships and a second failed marriage said to me that I'd had enough. My future plans included a comforting life with my animal partners and lots of good, nurturing contact with my women friends. Work would be my primary love and relationship. I had no need or want of new men for friendship or relationship. I wrote Fritz Saam that I would be out of town when he came through.

He responded, "I am disappointed that I won't be able to see you this time through, but I will wave as I pass through, knowing you are out there somewhere. Perhaps we will connect on my return trip. Any possibilities? We will meet someday. I will remain in touch."

I granted him a point for determination and put the

possibility of meeting out of my mind. Strongheart was the only male energy around my house, and that seemed enough. In truth, I was not eager to explore my discomfort with men nor ready to admit that I had never much trusted them. By design, nearly all of my animal companions had been female. The only reason that I had selected a male companion for Arrow was because I did not want her to feel any sense of competition with the feminine energy we had built and nurtured between us. Strongheart was the first and only male dog I'd ever invited into the family. My horse was a mare, my donkeys all jennies, the cats girls. Men, in general, were an enigma to me, and I strongly preferred the company of women and animals—preferably female animals.

As Lee and I struggled through our separation, I saw more and more reasons for putting what I called the "man-woman thing" behind me. My difficulty in establishing good boundaries made it far too easy to lose myself in relationships. I had never been very comfortable with men in any situation, and I felt alone in my own skin in intimate relationships. Lee and I had wounded each other enough in our painful efforts at intimacy. I would stick to Strongheart.

True to his word, Fritz wrote back a month later, again seeking a meeting and lunch. To this day I cannot say exactly why I said, "OK," but I did and then spent the rest of the day regretting it. When he called me later that week to make meeting arrangements, I was feeding my animals up at the barn. The barn phone was little used, and when I picked up the receiver, a cloud of dust wafted into my face. "Hello?" I coughed.

Fritz's voice on the line was businesslike and quiet and

bore no relationship to the voice I had come to imagine through his brief E-mail messages. It caught me a bit off guard. I had decided that if we were to meet, it would be at a restaurant. Letting him know where I lived would be foolish and risky. But when he said, "How do I get to you?" I automatically rattled off directions to my house, although he had not really even asked for them. When I hung up the phone, I was aghast. I swore at myself under my breath, cursing my stupidity. It was too much like me to collapse my barriers in the face of even a simple request. *Don't make waves. Accommodate. Do what is asked.* I had responded without thinking. Strongheart sprawled nearby watching me, a lazy grin on his face, his eyes at sleepy half-mast. I had certainly brought no honor that day to his good lessons on setting boundaries and keeping them.

My meeting with Fritz was scheduled for the next day, and I slept little that night. I had rebuilt the downstairs apartment and rented it to a lovely older couple who were building a home nearby. Early that next morning, I hurried to their door and asked them if they would hang around the house until midmorning, when Fritz was due. They offered to stay nearby and keep an eye and ear on things. Their assurances gave me a small measure of courage, and I breathed easier for the first time in twenty-four hours.

Fritz would be the first stranger to see my home in its near-completion. A burst of furious building energy on the part of my contractor saw most of the interior work on the house finished by mid-June. Outside, the new cedar siding was on the way to being freshly stained. Inside, the carpets and tile warmed the house with rich earth and straw colors, and my furniture and paintings had been miraculously cleaned, desmoked, and returned to me. Carpenters were still busy on trim and plumbing and seemingly endless other details, but the bulk of the work was finished, and all fingerprints of the fire had been wiped away. I kept one charred fence post in place to remind me of my fire journey and a photo of my burned house on the headboard above my pillow.

My hands had been busy replacing shrubs, spreading wildflower seed, and tending to the enchanted raspberry forest and the garden. In my journal I wrote stories of the resurrection of my home to engender a sense of homecoming. Although the work of maintaining the property on my own was beginning to overwhelm me, the house itself was far more beautiful than before the fire, and I had forged a tender new sense of home in the shelter of its walls.

I was hidden in the secret grove of the raspberry forest picking berries as large as my thumb when Fritz drove up in a large white truck and camper. Watching him from my enchanted hideaway, I felt as though I were looking out at real life from behind a curtain of dreams. A crow called over my head in a voice like churning gravel. Out into the sunlight I crawled, heading across the driveway as he stepped from the cab of his truck. My jeans were dirty, and I had leaves in my hair. Branches had torn holes in my old flannel shirt. He turned and extended his hand to me—a tan, callused hand that was uncommonly large—and said, "I'm Fritz."

I met his eyes, blue eyes like mine, and felt a rustling inside like a bird wing settle and go still. *This is safe*, I thought. The gods had protected me. My breath released, and I was surprised to find I had been holding it. "I'm Susan." Taking his hand, I shook it, and his grip was firm and sure. I can't abide mushy handshakes. At my invitation we headed toward the kitchen. For the next six hours, we talked. Sometimes our conversation came easily, like water cascading downhill. At other times we walked around our words like stiff-legged coyotes circling a perplexing scent.

My tenants came to the door on some flimsy pretense to check us out, heaven bless them. Then, seeing that I was alive and well, they left for an afternoon of golf. Fritz and I talked over coffee, over juice, over cookies. We talked on the porch outside and across the table from each other over lunch at Lily's Restaurant. We talked with Arrow stretched out at our feet and Strongheart's huge head resting in Fritz's lap. When the conversation began to ebb, we took a slow walk with the dogs up to the spring behind my house and listened to it trickle out of the concrete cistern onto a mound of brown creek stones.

Fritz watched the water as he spoke of his past two years on the road as a traveler, revisiting the Montana rivers of his boyhood, looking for a new life direction and a new home following the end of a long marriage. While he watched the water, I watched him. He was not a big man, slight actually, with a narrow torso and slender limbs. His eyes were very blue, his hair silver-white. While he talked, he twirled a twig in his thick fingers, and I was struck again at the size of his hands. *Like paws. Bear paws,* I told myself. Two years of mountain travel had weathered his face into a deep tan, and I found the whole of his countenance in its startling contrasts of white, blue, and brown something of a surprise.

Yes, that was a good word for my experience of him that day. He was a surprise to me. Our conversation, swinging from chatter about the dry summer weather to the meaning of travel and the paths of life and soul, was surprising in its depth and familiarity. Most surprising of all was the story he unraveled about the three-year journey he had taken to locate me and take me to lunch. I listened, transfixed, as he told about first reading my books and wanting to meet me, then discovering I had moved, then moved again. He had my E-mail address once, but it had changed. My publisher would not divulge my phone number but offered him an updated E-mail address, which had finally resulted in our meeting. In the course of those three years, we had both divorced and faced similar transitions. The fire had been my most recent resurrection from the ashes; two years of solitary travel were his.

By the time we walked back to the house, the afternoon shadows had grown long and blue. The dogs woofed in unison to remind me that it was dinnertime. Suddenly the day was over. I walked Fritz to his truck, and he gave me a brief, tight hug before he climbed in. Then he was gone, dust clouds dancing after the camper.

In my E-mail the next morning, I read, "Hi, Susan. It was great to finally meet you and have time to get to know you a bit. You are a busy lady but seem to have time for friendship. I will keep in touch. Thanks for keeping the door open.—Fritz"

Was I keeping the door open? I felt nervous and agitated. Part of me wanted to talk with him again, face-to-face, but another part of me wanted nothing of the sort. In the dreams I had been casting for myself since my separation, no room was included for a man. And the timing was horrible. I was only three months apart from Lee and had much healing to do. The animals all seemed more peaceful with the turmoil of the marriage strife gone from the house, and I felt that peace, too. I had set my course.

But for all my misgivings, I found myself telling my friends about the enigmatic man who had seemed to fall out of the sky and land on my doorstep, and when Fritz wrote that he was coming back through my part of the world again in August, I made time to meet with him. As before, I spent the next few days regretting my decision, wanting nothing more than to run away and hide under a log. The morning of his visit, I got up, washed my hair, laid out my newest overalls, and put on lipstick for the first time in recent memory. *What in the world are you doing??* I asked myself. *This is not a date!* When he showed up on my doorstep, he had a mischievous smile on his face and a large box in his hands. *Those hands. How can anyone have such big hands?*

"I found this for you at a shop in Missoula, Montana," he said, handing over the box. "I followed my instincts. I don't know why, but it just felt right. Like it was something you would understand." I untied the raffia bow and opened the box. Pulling aside the crisp white tissue, I found myself face-to-face with a large, primitive outline of an elk head that had been woven into a soft, gray wool blanket. The room seemed to spin, and my heart caught in my throat. *My elk,* I thought. *My protector and my teacher. This man brought me an elk robe.* I looked up at Fritz, stunned. "You don't know what this means to me." My voice was very small and sounded far-away to me, and I pressed the soft wool of the blanket hard between my fingers. He smiled broadly, yet I knew he could not possibly understand the significance of what he had brought to my door. I couldn't understand it completely myself.

"I just knew you would like it," he said, obviously pleased with himself. "I had a felt sense about it." *Felt sense.* It was a phrase I used often from a tiny book called *Focusing*.[1] I thought I was the only person alive who had read it.

When he left later that afternoon, after hours of good talk, it was too soon. I was wanting more conversation, and more of him and his company. When he put his hands to my shoulders and embraced me in a quick good-bye hug, it felt good to be held in those large hands, like being in the grip of a warm bear hug. It felt safe. His chest was hard and comforting, and I could hear his breathing. He pulled back, but I didn't, and so, momentarily startled, he pulled me close one more time. When at last he backed away, he looked at me closely, a question behind his blue eyes. "I'll be seeing you again." It was all he said as he silently climbed into his truck and drove away north, back to the parks, the rivers, and the mountains.

In the weeks that followed, Fritz began a daily ritual of E-mail messages to me as he traveled into the northern mountains. The effect of his letters was startling. I found them both invasive and compelling. Each day I eagerly awaited them, at the same time fearing what they might contain.

"Susan, I enjoyed our time together so much. It was nourishing. You are a very special person to me, and I am aware that we have grown quite close in the short times we have spent together. Why do people cross our paths and enter our lives? The answers are still unfolding. What is it I have to learn from you, and you from me? —Fritz"

Writing was a solitary, intensely personal venture for me, one I had never imagined might also be a partnership of exploration between two people. But as the E-mails from Fritz came and deepened, and I wrote back in answer, the mystery of words on paper took on a new and fresh meaning for me. I began to sense the wonder in this new mode of intimate dialogue. In *Soul Mates*, Thomas Moore writes, "Something happens to our thoughts and emotions when we put them into a letter; they are then not the same as spoken words. They are placed in a different, special context, and they speak at a different level, serving the soul's organ of rumination rather than the mind's capacity for understanding."[2]

I found the truth of Moore's reflections as Fritz and I exchanged mail over many weeks. It was a new kind of dialogue and a new way of listening. The written word is magical, spoken without sound yet clear in its meaning, much as a sharp smell must be to an animal with a fine nose: a language delivered not through the ear but through the deeper feeling places of the body. For years I had spoken to an unseen public in this language that had become sacred to me. Now someone was speaking back, clearly, insistently, and regularly.

When I call to mind that first series of letters we exchanged, they are attended by the smell of smoke, as though the letters themselves were burning. The summer of 2000, when our E-mails were at a peak, the mountain West exploded in a series of fires. Unusually dry summer weather and equally unusual high winds fueled fires and firestorms that burned 1.2 million acres in the Rocky Mountains and a total of 6.8 million acres nationwide. It was the worst fire season in fifty years.

One hot and stifling night in August, I thrashed in bed, sleepless and agitated until morning. When first light came, I saw the haze in the sky over the Salt River Range. By sunup the haze had become a brownish, billowing cloud, and the familiar smell of smoke stung my nostrils. Balancing on the thin edge between sleep and wakefulness, my body had told me what my mind had missed the night before: fire was raging in the canyons a scant twenty miles away. I began saturating the grounds around my house.

That morning Fritz wrote, "The entire area—West Yellowstone, Bozeman, and Ennis, Montana—is completely covered in smoke. There are fires in every direction, and there is simply no escaping the smoke clouds. It is the worst I have ever seen. I am trying to come to terms with the fact that there are fires and smoke everywhere I want to go. . . . How is the smoke situation in your area?"

His words struck home with me: "There are fires and smoke everywhere I want to go." That was certainly the case in my life, on every level. I wondered if the fires that chased him were metaphorical as well.

As if reading my mind, he wrote me that night, "I continue on my journey north. I look forward to the day when I once again have some roots. I have a terrible ungrounded feeling, which keeps me on edge a lot. I don't have a home right now, and that is hard to swallow. You can sense my sadness and grief bubbling out. There must be a meaning to this traveling. The search for myself goes on. It is lonely out here."

The next day flames chased David out of Greys River Canyon as he was making preparations there for the yearly Cherokee Green Corn Dance ceremony. We held the four-day Corn Dance at David's house instead, keeping the sacred fire burning in a barbecue and heating the stones for the sweat lodges on a propane camp stove to comply with local fire bans on private property. Smoke covered the valley, and we coughed as we danced, offering not only our thanksgiving prayers but prayers for an end to the fires.

At the Corn Dance, I thought of Fritz and of fire, and of my fears of relationship, which licked around my ankles like the orange flames that rose from the depths of the canyons.

I wrote to him, "Fritz, I want to see you. And I want to take it slow. You are compelling to me, and you scare me to death. I have lots of fears that are nameless and smothering. I have intense fears about getting close. I don't know why this is all so threatening to me—maybe I brought it in from another lifetime."

He responded, "You have leaped into a brave new world. I will catch you with open arms. You are safe with me. And yes, I know it will take time. But I have lots of it. Your courage to be a little more vulnerable is wise. Your vulnerability is not your weakness. It is your strength. You must be courageous—and I must be, too."

I had asked to be the firekeeper for that year's Corn Dance ceremony, taking responsibility for the sacred fire that burned round the clock for four days. In this way I wanted to honor the spirit of fire, which had directed so much of my life for the previous year. I had no idea when I made the request that fire was not through with me yet. As I sat in front of the tiny flames sizzling in the bottom of the barbecue and watched the orange glow in the night sky over Greys River, I wondered if I would ever get a rest between blazes.

Pulling the elk blanket from Fritz around my shoulders for comfort, I let my mind tentatively explore the unsettled discomfort I had been living with since Fritz's first letter to me. The image of a tiny snake came to mind. I followed the mental photo back to its origin, to where it had rested in true life, coiled furtively in a shallow hole dug in the sand.

I was ten years old, on a day trip with my friend Ann
and her family. We were playing by the shores of a river,
when I heard young voices shouting and yelling. Looking
over the heads of a crowd of children, I saw three boys of
about twelve standing around a hole in the sand. One of
them held a large rock over his head. In the hole was a tiny
snake, no longer than a pencil and as slender as a pipe
cleaner. The girls in the crowd were screeching and hiding
their faces in their hands, and the other boys were shouting
to the three, "Do it! Do it! Smash it!"

To this day I cannot describe the horror and shock that
attended that moment for me. Heart thudding in my ears,
bile welling up in my throat, I stared pop-eyed at the tiny,
helpless snake, who looked up at all of us with eyes like
sparkling black stars. The commotion level rose, with children yelling and screeching around me. Meanwhile mothers
and fathers sunbathed at the river's edge, behaving as
though what was going on ten feet from them was invisible.
My head was spinning so badly I was getting dizzy. Some
power unknown to me moved my legs, and I bolted forward,
shoving children aside with my elbows and hands. Reaching
the boy with the rock, I screamed out at him to let the snake
alone in a voice that croaked and broke with emotion. He
told me to get lost, pushed me out of the way, and raised the
rock higher.

In utter desperation I balled up my fist and socked him
as hard as I could in the stomach—the first and only person
I have ever struck in my life. He doubled over with a loud
"Ooof," and the rock fell in the sand. I grabbed the snake
from its would-be grave, blubbering loudly, my face contorted in anguish and snot running down my chin. In the

cups of my hands, the snake wiggled as I ran and ran and kept on running, down the river to where the crowds vanished and the silence finally surrounded me. Kneeling down, I opened my fingers and watched the reptile uncurl from its protective coil, its skin smooth as summer against my palms as it slid silently away into the river grass.

The river water felt ice-cold when I splashed it on my face, wiping away the tears and the dirt. My braids were full of burrs and twigs, and my legs were scratched and sore. For a moment I sat along the banks, breathing heavily. My hands shook. When I finally walked back to my group, a surprise awaited me that would forever alter the way I viewed the world.

I was asked to apologize to the boy I had hit. The request struck me like a bucket of gasoline thrown in my face. That moms and dads—the lawmakers in my child world— had stood by and done nothing while they watched a group of children prepare to kill a harmless creature had alarmed me. That they did not offer to step in when I was shoved roughly aside had frightened and confused me. That other little girls—my gender sisters—had watched the event behind shielded eyes and screamed and tittered and also done nothing was a further affront to my senses. But to be told to apologize to the "killer" was the final outrage. *Why? What else could I have done? They were going to kill the snake!* I couldn't grasp any of what was happening.

Well, I was told, I had acted out of line. Violence could not be tolerated. *What about the violence being committed against the snake?* It was just a snake.

Ann's parents felt the defiance in me, and so did the parents of the redheaded bully boy, a youth whose eyes I refused to meet as I muttered my most insincere "sorry" to him through clenched teeth. *Don't make waves. Accommodate. Do what is asked.* This was a lesson I would hear over and over again.

When I was six, I had been given my very first pet—a lovely, calico, longhaired guinea pig. At the time we lived in a trailer park, and the landlord, Mr. Bolt, who was a mean-spirited, heavy-drinking cuss of a man, came after me and my animal friend with a set of long-handled garden shears, threatening to chop off the head of my new companion. I screamed and told him to go away, that he was a nasty and mean man, and I ran home to the safety of my mother. Instead of comforting me in my moment of horror, Mom made me apologize to Mr. Bolt. Then she confined me to the trailer for the rest of the afternoon and made me go to bed early as punishment for speaking rudely to an adult. Years later she told me that she was afraid of Mr. Bolt. He could have made us leave the trailer court at a time when we had no money to move anywhere, but she said nothing of that at the time, and maybe that was right. I don't know.

Instead, I heard only that I was to take what I knew to be true—that Mr. Bolt was a son of a bitch—and swallow it and make nice. *Don't make waves. Accommodate. Do what is asked.* In this way we teach our children to stuff the gift of their intuition and thus deaden their ability to discriminate between what is morally right and wrong, what is safe and not. Two days later Mr. Bolt told my parents to get rid of the guinea pig or pay an enormous amount of extra rent. The true reason, plain and simple, was because Mr. Bolt was a bum, but I believed that it was because I had made waves, and I cried myself to sleep for weeks after my dad took "Squeaky" back to the pet shop. I had learned my lesson. The snake experience just solidified it. I learned how to swallow a lot.

My experience with the snake and my guinea pig taught me, too, something about men—something I would take to heart for life. These were not the only experiences I had in which the male sex seemed to take a certain glee in harming or threatening life. Growing up, I saw boys blow up crickets with firecrackers, tie rubber bands around the tails of terrified cats until the tails decomposed and fell off, and perform many other "childhood pranks" upon helpless animals that were not pranks to me but assaults against spirit. In my later years in humane work, I saw more cruelty cases than I want to count, cases uglier and more evil than I care to discuss. Most always, with rare exceptions, the perpetrators were boys or men.

I put together my snake and guinea pig experiences in a way that made sense to my child mind: boys and men could hurt and threaten life. They could do so with the "lawmakers' "—or parents'—approval. The law and the lawmakers could not be trusted to do what was just. And as I grew older, it did not escape my notice that those who made the laws and enforced them were mostly men.

In a convoluted twist of life and circumstance, and my interpretation of them both, men became suspicious in my eyes because of the very personal and painful experiences I had with them surrounding animals. As I grew older and restoration of the Earth became important to me, again, it seemed that men wielded and used a deadly power to destroy nature.

Because of my early, effective training in deadening my inner sense of what was right and what was safe, I also came to mistrust *myself* in my interactions with men. More than once on dates, I found myself in stressful, occasionally frightening, situations because of my overwillingness to accommodate and not make waves. My caution threshold had been turned down too low. And it was easier to blame men for the sometimes alarming turn of events than face my own mistrust and betrayal of myself.

Animals remained a safe haven for me, as I know they do for many people. As an animal lover, I've heard nearly all of the sarcastic remarks that disparage those who seem to love animals more than people, but I do not believe one loves animals more than humankind. Rather, many of us—especially women—feel safer with our animal kin than with humankind, and perhaps particularly with mankind.

Poet Judith Collas writes of a woman who wishes she "were sleeping with the right man instead of with her dog,/but she never felt she was sleeping with the wrong dog."[3] We women read this and giggle. Yet just under the surface of this light poem of men and dogs boils a foaming, turbulent ocean of truth about those men to whom we ache to trust our bodies in sleep and in wakefulness. I don't know where other women seed and grow their guardedness with men, but I know it is there, lurking just beneath all of the flippant and cruel "men jokes" we women tell ourselves and one another. To this day I continue to search for more of the puzzle pieces of my own pain and withholding: a tiny snake is just one of them. And, yes, I have slept with the wrong men and never with the wrong dog.

In September, when the fires in Greys River Canyon were still smoldering and smoke along the mountain highways had settled into his lungs and given him a raging respiratory infection, Fritz came back to visit me. We had logged hundreds of E-mails between us that ran from the most casual to the quietly intimate. This time he stayed four days, parking his camper in my driveway, coming in to share meals, conversations, and evenings by the woodstove. The dogs adored him, following at his heels for attention, and he was as gentle with all my animal family as any man I'd ever seen. He was equally gentle with me. And he was eager to know me better and for us to get closer in every way. I remained as furtive as a chipmunk in a woodpile, darting in and out of hiding, cautious to the extreme at revealing my true and unguarded self in any way. My insides felt knotted. I said to him, "Having you here in the house is like having you inside of me. This house is me. I don't know what to do."

On the fourth day, I woke up from a brief afternoon nap with the fluttering in my stomach calm at last. Something had shifted, and I felt at peace. I walked into the kitchen and found a note on the kitchen counter. Fritz had gone.

He called me from the road that evening, a quick call just to say that the tension had become too much and he needed to get away and sort his thoughts. His voice sounded shaky and lost, and he hurried off the phone, telling me just before he hung up that he would write. The irony of it swept over me. I had only just felt safe enough to consider coming out of hiding, and he had left! My first reaction was anger, then mistrust. *He let me down. He ran. He won't be here for me.*

That evening he wrote, "I feel sheepish sitting here after running away. I just needed some time to myself to make sense out of all that is going on. I ask myself, Is this relationship possible? Am I in your face too much? Am I too intense? Should I pull back and be circumspect and uninvolved, or should I just sit down and cry?"

I answered, "I feel a bit defeated by our circumstances. It feels overwhelming right now and intense—often too intense. This is my home and my life you are stepping into. I have no opportunity to leave mine and step into yours for a while. You are a traveler for the time being. Fritz, you have been living in risky emotional space, alone for more than a year now. There is a lot of risk with us, too. I fear we will burn either too fast or too bright and burn out."

Our voices through the mail were startlingly different from the ones we used face-to-face. The printed word gave us an honesty and a directness that we could not find in words spoken aloud to each other. The tiny marks of black ink on white paper seemed to me like the tracks of animals in fresh snow: clear, precise, honest, real. And like tracks, they led us down a path of their own. Stress management consultant Ann Sturgis writes of her own experience with this kind of radical, written dialogue: "In the process of writing to someone, which is a solitary endeavor, there exists the possibility of drawing from one's most creative, expressive depths. In this space, we know what feels important to say, and we can reach forth into the life of another to know that other and to be known."[4]

While I carried on at home with the animals and the house and Fritz wandered the greater Yellowstone region, the E-mails between us continued. The daily writing was a unique, often turbulent experience. More than once we said good-bye to each other, only to write again a day later. Although it seemed as though we were leaving nothing unsaid, I was keeping my anger at his leaving me so abruptly out of the meandering tracks of our words. It seemed a stupid sentiment for me to hold and far more reactive than the

212 • Heart in the Wild

situation between us seemed to call for. After all, he was merely a visitor, a friend of sorts, who was certainly free to leave at will.

Two weeks went by and the words continued, keeping open a fresh trail of crisp footprints between us. "Journaling connects us to something more than our little ego identity that can be buffeted about like a small boat at sea," Ann wrote me. "If we reach forth to another in writing with serious intent, there is the possibility of a union of I and thou. Spirit moves through our words and our intentions to greet and affirm the Otherness of our correspondent."[5]

The words between Fritz and me had tamped down a well-worn path, like a narrow, smooth game trail that winds in dark woods, forging impossible openings through deep brush and boggy quagmires. From the grounding of that thin, sharp-curved, branch-laden trail, Fritz let go a message to me with the force of an arrow winging through thin mountain air: "This is a heavy question for me to ask and maybe for you to answer. Susan, does the fact that you had serious cancer several times have anything to do with your fears of closeness? I ask this in all sincerity.—Fritz"

His question found a true and sudden home in the confusion I had been courting over why his leaving struck me so hard and so painfully. I sat up late that night and, under a sky brilliant with autumn stars, wrote back: "It has a lot to do with how I view intimate partners, Fritz. I am concerned about partnering with people who may not know how to do such a difficult walk with a person. When I went through that challenge in my life, those closest to me were terrified, and in many ways I took that walk alone. I am fearful cancer might come back someday. I would rather face it alone than in a partnership that could leave me feeling alone, which is the worst of experiences. Fritz, you left me."

There, I said it.

"And you left me with no warning. I woke up, and you were gone. Are you the kind of man who can walk through fire with me, or will I always have to be afraid that when I go to sleep, I will wake up and find you gone?" I turned off my computer and went to bed, my anger flowing off me like rainwater from having expressed it on paper.

When I awoke early the next morning to the sound of flickers pecking holes in my fence post, Fritz had already written: "Oh, Susan, a wave of emotion washes over me after reading your letter. Your courage is great and your trust well placed. Tears stream down my face. . . . In the past I have always had the option of leaving to take time for myself when I needed to sort things out. I thought it was a useful strategy for a long time, but it wasn't, and it hurt the people around me. I can see now that the time for that is past. I will not run away anymore. I will not. Many men are undone by a woman's illness. Carl Jung said it is the greatest challenge facing men—to be able to be present to a woman's pain. Somehow I know that I would not be undone by yours, that I could be there for you should the time ever come. Because of your bout with cancer, you are immeasurably stronger. Now is the time to be softer. The substance of our relationship is mighty. We are bound by something deep and powerful. . . . I love you."

Three days later we met in town for the first time in several weeks. Despite all his young years in Montana, Fritz had never heard the bugling of rutting elk, and they were once again in full chorus in Teton Park. I had invited him to go with me to one of my favorite spots near an old abandoned ranch where bull elk always seemed to congregate. He had sprouted a beard since I'd last seen him, snow-white like his hair, and looked even more tan than I had remembered. When we walked down the grassy game trail toward the woods, he reached for my hand, and we walked along in silence. A flock of geese flew across the face of a big moon, their rough voices speaking of crackling leaves and cold nights. The air was fresh and rippling with energy.

I had planned on a snowy white winter, bedded down in my heart's home with a woman caretaker to help me manage the workload, with my mother in residence, with Strongheart and Arrow, Polani and Aurora and Fashion. I had planned a life under the umbrella of safe and secure women's energy, one that did not include "looking again" at a vision of me partnered with any man. I had framed a life for myself that I dreamed would resist the timeless calling to passionate union of the mystery of male and female. But under the stars that night, surrounded by the haunting whistle of elk music all around me, a long-forgotten memory of Elk and Elk magic floated down like a dusting of yellow pine pollen and covered my shoulders. And I remembered Elk as the spirit that enraptures and captivates, as the flute player of irresistible, seductive charm.

A herd of cow elk barked in the darkness of the open meadow before me and suddenly charged across the bent, yellow grasses, like a giant river running. Rolling Thunder had spoken of right timing, how it has to be experienced to be understood. *Sometimes,* I thought, with an odd mixture of melancholy and joy juggling for space in my heart, *right timing is not the timing you would have chosen. Rather, the timing chooses you, sweeps you away like a crisp yellow leaf on the night wind.* Fritz held my face in his callused hands and put his lips on mine. *Like flower petals,* I thought. When he finally pulled away, I said, "Come home with me."

And he said yes.

12

Mitaku Oyasin
(All My Relations)

*Separate and together, we are born of mystery into
mystery, expressions of a single miracle. It lives in the raccoon's
quick paws and lively strength, in the bear's glance and the red squirrel
gripping the limb, in the cries of the coyotes, the gaze of the deer, in the
honeybee's dance. It swims in rivers and sea, flies on wings through
the ocean of air, it stirs in the stillness of the forest night
—it burns in the screech owl and it burns in me, the same fire,
the same brief fire, shining from eyes to other eyes.*
—John Daniel, *The Trail Home*

In October, when the aspen trees had turned gold and
the forest fires still smoldered in the West awaiting the
snows that would eventually douse them, I took myself on a
three-day vision quest into Teton Park. It was time to ac-
knowledge—now that the house was rebuilt, my divorce behind me, and my new book in the works—that I was
stepping onto a path of new beginnings. Following a forest
fire, it is the rising of green shoots that signals rebirth after

217

the seeds have "cooked" underground for a length of time. I had been cooking my seeds in the soil of introspection for many, many months. The time had come to see what the new growth was going to look like and to say prayers for this fresh start in my life.

David told me to choose a place that was sacred to me, and I chose the woods near Ox Bow Bend on the Snake River. Fritz canoed me across the river at dawn to my vision place, and I walked into the forest with my sleeping bag, tarp, and David's family staff covered with eagle and hawk feathers. With me, too, was the ceremonial pipe David had given me the year before, which I had been using regularly in personal ceremonies since then.

These three days were to be days of reflection, of thanksgiving for all of life's gifts to me, and of prayers for myself and for "the people," which included human, animal, plant, and mineral people and the air, water, fire, and earth people—"Mitaku Oyasin," or "all my relations." As I prayed for the people, David told me, the people would watch over me, protect me, and bring me lessons and wisdom and perhaps even a vision.

I waved good-bye to Fritz at the shore of the river, and he paddled away into a white mist that hung over the water. Carrying my belongings into the woods, I found a natural glen surrounded by pines and carpeted in yellow grass. Morning sun filtered down through the trees, and birds whistled above me. In the center of the glen were the bones of an elk, which I believed had drawn me to make my vision circle in this special place. Using sage I had picked at home and handfuls of elk bones, I made a circle at one end of the glen and unrolled my sleeping bag and elk blanket in the center of it. Then I sat down. Hours passed. The autumn sun climbed overhead. Flies droned around me. The swoosh of big wings above me signaled three sandhill cranes flying east.

Praying for a while, meditating, staring, shifting my body weight to keep from cramping, swishing a never-ending train of ants off my legs, I realized that three days seemed like an endless amount of time to be sitting in a glen of bones. Minutes were passing like days. Never in my life had I sat in one place for so long being still. At home I never passed an hour away without busying myself in some fashion, with the animals, the yard, the house. By midday I was fidgeting and restless. By late afternoon I was anxious and bored.

By early evening something else had started stirring in me: as the prospect of night loomed ahead, a flicker of panic began tapping at me from inside my chest walls. The moon was as thin as a string, promising little light. The trees were tall around me and dense as smoke. I was facing a night alone in a way that I had never been alone before. This was not a campground with soothing human sounds or a neighborhood where streetlights burned the dark away and phones were within the reach of fingertips. Fritz, home, and friends were forty miles away. I didn't even have my precious dogs to comfort me. I thought about the black bear we had been told was in the immediate area.

As the sun set behind the Tetons and the daylight faded, my panic increased commensurately with the coming of the dark. By the time the light was gone, I was huddled in my sleeping bag, nearly breathless with fear. The stars rose like sparkling bits of glass, but I was too terrified to poke my head out of my bag to watch them. Every soft sound of a twig snapping or a bit of grass moving threw me into fits of shuddering so intense I could almost hear my teeth clatter. I could not look out for fear of what I would see out there. *What would I see out there?* Dark trees, a still night, maybe the shadow of an owl. Life going on about its business.

With shame I thought of my anger at the early settlers who had proclaimed wilderness fearful and bad. That night, in the safety of a national park, I descended into a blacker kind of wilderness than I imagined had ever been conceived by the most mortified of pioneers. In the dark of the night, the animals I treasured as teachers and healers suddenly no longer seemed like my relations. I think if a curious vole had scooted over my sleeping place, I might have died of fright. So deep was my dread, I almost could not move.

Far away I heard a sound like gusting wind. It came again, then again, louder each time. Through the fog of my panicked stupor, I finally recognized the sound for what it was—thunder. Propelled from my sleeping bag by a blast of lightning, I fumbled with my tarp, wrapping it around my sleeping bag as the first large drops of rain splattered onto the plastic with a sound like tiny gunshots. I dived back into the bag as another lightning flash lit up the sentinel wall of trees around me and a sheet of wind roared through the glen.

Rain slapped my tarp, and rolling thunder boomed from all directions, drowning out every other night sound. In the darkness with the tarp pulled over my head, I prayed for the storm to last through the night. The lightning was a friend fighting back the darkness, and the roaring boom of the storm, a noise that flooded out the voice of panic between my ears. That my bag was growing soggy bothered me little. The idea of dark silence was far worse.

The storm eventually receded despite my fervent prayers

and moved off across the prairies and autumn-gold mountains to light up other night-wild landscapes. I heard it leave, a sound like fading hoofbeats, and my heart ached with longing. The darkness returned, even blacker now that the stars had been blotted away by clouds, which covered the sky like a thick membrane.

That night was the longest of my life. I had once believed that no night could have been longer than the one following my cancer diagnosis, but I was wrong. The night of my diagnosis had been one of bottomless despair. Still, despair was a kinder companion than the fear that clutched at me with ragged and insistent claws. Counting each second of darkness as I searched desperately for the first tint of light in the eastern sky, I risked a cautious glance into a landscape far more menacing than the dark outside: I looked within.

With a start of sudden insight, I realized that I had known the contours of certain inlets of this murky, water-like fear all my life. Flowing unseen beneath the surface of my days and nights, this fear as old as mountains and as deep as the sky slept in me like a huge, underground lake. Meeting it in the forest had forced me to recognize it. And I *did* recognize it. Now that the whole of the fear was before me, I could sense its influence in every corner of my life. What choices had I made to keep the fear underground? What jobs had I taken and kept, what moves had I made, what pass-times had I busied myself with, what relationships had I involved myself in to keep from facing that deep, nameless, dreaded dark? I wondered, too, how many people lived feeling the bitter intensity of such fear at every moment, in broad daylight, surrounded by distraction and busyness. I believe now that I have met many of them, and I have a far greater respect for their circumstances than I had previously embraced.

By the time the sky to the east was not so much light as perhaps a fraction less black, I had learned a powerful lesson about myself: I was a woman who walked with fear. I could not banish or even name the fear or locate its true origin, but that was not as important as knowing that it was with me, touching me, directing me whether I named it or not, recognized it or not, spoke with it or not. This fear was a part of me that could not be put away or outgrown, just as flesh and bones cannot be outgrown until we die. Rather, it remained an honest, true part of me that would never cease inviting my exploration and reflection. My humility grown suddenly large, I had discovered yet another dimension of myself as a woman afraid of an unnameable dark. It was not the new beginning I had imagined finding in the forest, but it was a beginning nonetheless.

The forest was soft-bottomed with rain, and droplets of water hung from the huckleberry bushes like fine pear-drop crystals. Barefoot, I carried my pipe to the riverbank and loaded it, offering a pinch of tobacco to the spirits of the four directions, to Mother Earth, to Father Sky, and to all my relations, as David had taught me. As I prayed and smoked, the gift of the morning unfolded on the river. A lone white pelican drifted toward me on huge black-tipped wings and landed on the glassy surface of the emerald waters. Three moose ambled in the willows on the opposite shore. A deer forded a shallow spot downstream on legs like tender branches. Two bald eagles circled overhead, their voices as soft and musical as wind chimes.

Normally rising much later in the day, I had missed the

magic of dawn nearly all of my life. And it was not a thing to be missed: the silent loveliness took my breath away as fully as my panic had the night before. But this breathlessness was not born of fear. Instead, it had been birthed in beauty—beauty in its most tender color, exquisite stillness, and uninhibited expression. Morning birds began singing up the sun all around me. Fish rose, sending out concentric ripples on the water as gangly-legged water bugs skated near the river's edge.

Beauty, like the sense of belonging and the majesty of transcendent moments, is a part of the trinity of universal experience that transforms lives. On the river I understood with my body that beauty is far more than pleasant aesthetic and that wild landscape is more than a "Kodak moment." Wildland, merely the look of it, is a vital component of Earth's natural medicine to us. Beauty has the power to heal. Perhaps much of the healing that animals had brought to my life came from the simple beauty of their form and color and how delicately, surely, and gracefully they moved in the world. I thought of the ancient tradition of the Japanese tea ceremony, in which every movement is executed with long-studied grace and precision, and in the morning unraveling before me, I witnessed that same measure of beauty and gracefulness. Mesmerized, I sat still and watched the morning unfold. *Unfold.* When had I ever let anything in my life just unfold in its natural order, without cranking the direction, the timing, and the pace?

As the creatures and the elements of the day danced together—the sunlight, the soft breath of morning breeze, the moose and birds and deer—I noticed, too, how slowly the world moved outside of my human domain. The moose trio meandered through the willows in slow motion on ash-colored legs. Eagles made lazy, unhurried circles in the sky. Ripples drifted out from the rising fish in sleepy, widening rings. Only the singing birds sounded busy or hurried. Clouds floated slowly, slowly above me. *Is this the rhythm of the Earth? Is this the pace we were meant to keep? Is this why I feel so crazy in my life at home, running all the time, keeping pace with cars and clocks and computers? Am I meant to live on moose time? On cloud time?*

A young beaver swam around the bend in the river and headed straight toward my side of the bank. I could see his broad, webbed feet paddling in slow strokes, his fat tail floating out behind him like a raft. Reaching the bank, he stretched his paws up onto shore and ambled up onto the gravel bar not five feet from me. I could have reached out and touched his dripping fur, his stone-gray tail. His eyes were small and round, set wide apart on a face I can only describe as innocent, harmless. I knew he could not miss seeing me. I sat like a huge, breathing boulder right beside him.

As he slowly settled himself into a sitting posture, he gazed into my face, head weaving from side to side. For a long time, he squatted like an old Buddha figure, back humped, head forward, hands clasped thoughtfully in front of his chest. Then he pulled his eyes from mine and began grooming himself. With paws the color of coffee, he wiped the water away from his face. He scratched his wide back, his legs, his neck, and his tiny ears with slow deliberation and licked the water drops off his tail. With an audible sigh, he stretched out on the bank, rolled in the sand, and stared at the water. His whole demeanor was nothing like what I had imagined of a beaver. *Aren't you supposed to be busy?* I asked him silently. *Aren't beavers always busy? Isn't there a dam somewhere that needs your attention?*

His actions answered me: *There is "busy," and there is "crazy." Sister, you work like crazy. There is no point in it. Sit, watch, rest. The work will all get done in good time.* The beaver brought to my mind the famous last words of the great avatar Meher Baba: "Don't worry, be happy." Surely, if the beaver could speak, those would be his words as well. We sat silently together for several more minutes, and then my friend launched himself back into the river, smacking his tail on the surface before diving and vanishing into the morning.

I returned reluctantly to my hidden glen of bones. Even though it had seemed welcoming the previous morning, it suddenly felt foreboding. The tall, tight circle of trees that had seemed so sheltering to me now felt suffocating. Whether it was because I had contaminated the place with my fear or because I was not welcomed there, I did not know. By leaving the glen with my pipe that morning, I had already broken the rules David set for me, which were to stay in one place and sit. After hours of deliberation, fear had the final word, driving me out of the glen with my belongings. Wandering a scant twenty yards north to where I could see water, I set up another hidden camp and settled down for the evening. I did not return to the glen of bones for the rest of my vision quest.

That night passed more easily. The sight of water shining like a nickel in the starlight brought me comfort. I was still deeply afraid, but not shiveringly so. Still, I counted the minutes until daybreak, once again returning to the riverbank to smoke my pipe and pray. Again the pelican came swooshing in on cloudlike wings to break the silent surface of the river. Again, the moose, eagles, deer, and beaver visited. And again, they all moved so slowly, so beautifully, a ballet choreographed by a transcendent master.

By the end of the day, the very beginnings of a change in my own rhythm had seeded in me, and I knew I would carry home a new way of moving in the world that had more to do with unfolding and less to do with crazy busyness. My third night ended in a rainstorm. Again, I was fearful, but the fear seemed bearable. By the time Fritz paddled across the river to carry me back home the next day, I was both eager and sorry to leave.

My brief days in the forest carried profound meaning for me. David had told me they would, but I could not understand until I had experienced them. There is a mystery—and at the same time a simple practicality—in sitting in solitude for several days. It is something few people ever do, yet it remains a ritual in nearly every spiritual tradition. Now I can understand why. When we are alone, voices we seldom hear and often don't want to hear can come to visit and make peace with us. Some of these are our inner voices. Some are the wise and ancient voices of Mitaku Oyasin. A vision quest or solitary retreat gives all these voices their due.

When I told David about my experience in the forest, and particularly in the glen, he asked me if I had asked the bones of the elk if they would help me or if I had simply gathered them up. Sheepishly I had to admit that I had just grabbed them. "I thought so," he said. "In doing that, you did not honor them. You were disrespectful to the grave site of the elk, and the elk is angry. That is the fear you felt. Elk medicine is strong in your life, and it is good medicine. You need to make peace with the bones." David told me to go back, to pray and speak to the bones, and to make offerings to them of tobacco, cornmeal, and a giveaway of some kind. Then he told me to ask for help from the trees, the grass, the stones, from everything in the glen, and spend one more night there. "It will be different if you do it this way. You'll see. The fear will leave, and you will feel the comfort of all your relations that move in the forest at night, instead of feeling afraid of them. You forgot to ask them for help."

Before the first snows, I went back and made my prayers and my offerings and found that David was quite correct. While I still recognized the lake of fear that resided within me and had always resided in me, I felt at peace with Elk once again.

Winter snows came in November, and the land was blanketed deep by Thanksgiving. I had much to be thankful for that year. My home was warm, comforting, and complete. Lee and I were forging a good friendship. The animals and I were healthy. I had a caretaker on board to help with the house and animal chores. My new book was under way. Most of all, I had Fritz, who was my most unexpected gift and a source of fresh wonder and delight every day.

In addition, I was thankful beyond words for a small group of regular winter visitors. Three bull elk—a five-point, a six-point, and a seven-point—had been trooping out of the aspens each evening in a stately line. Their trail was well worn and led straight to the front of my barn. Every night I could count on a vision of their absolute wild beauty unfolding beneath the floodlight of the barn door. The elk had turned color from summer brown to winter gray, and their legs were the rich, deep hue of mink. From their heads massive antlers sprouted like trees, and their furry rump patches were the color of moonglow.

It took only the sight of their antlers rising above the hill to usher me into sacred space, or spiritual time. The elk were magic to me and their visitations a lovely nighttime ritual of deep yet unnameable significance. I felt so blessed by their presence, imagining that perhaps they had chosen my home, my pastures, and in doing so had anointed me or blessed me in some special way. Elk magic and elk medicine had meant so much to me over the past year. Elk had bugled for me for years and had visited me in my shamanic journey and in meditative visits after the fire. Fritz had come to my door with an elk robe, and elk bones had graced the site of my vision quest. The lessons from Elk had been enduring and were seemingly endless. Without question Elk had indeed been my protector and my teacher. Now I had the added glory of their regular nighttime visits.

Of the four horses in our pasture, Fashion, my mare, was most at ease with them and would generously share her hay pile without complaint. The elk rarely made any aggressive moves toward the horses, and everyone seemed to get along just fine. Although it is highly frowned upon by park and forestry officials, I started leaving hay out by the barn for them, so that they would eat less of the horses'. Each evening, as I scattered out three flakes of grass hay and a scant scoop of grain, I would call out loud to where "the fellows" rested on the hillside, asking them to please continue to share. "If this is going to work," I called, "you have to share with the horses." Always they did. On Thanksgiving evening I placed a full bale of hay out for them, setting the flakes in a full circle like a medicine wheel, and sprinkling sage on top. Offering a prayer of thanks to the Creator for the visitations of the elk, I asked also for their safety that winter.

One morning not long afterward, I awoke to the sound of gunshots outside. Running into the driveway, I saw the three elk bounding up the hillside, while my neighbor fired a shotgun into the air. The elk had visited his barn that night, and he was not as happy with the visits as I was. Remembering the horror of my elk who had been run down with snow machines the previous winter, I was determined to do whatever I could to keep my three elk safe. I felt a sense of responsibility for the elk's welfare, as I do for any wild animal that comes onto my property. Since childhood I have felt this peculiar urgency to mother or keep safe any creature that crosses my path.

My beautiful bull elk of the previous winter had been taken away because the neighborhood would not give away. We were stingy with our hay, our belongings, and were unwilling to meet the elk halfway in making safe and respectful space for all of us. Surely, I told myself, it could be different than that. There had to be a way to live in peace with three elk. As if to drive the challenge even closer to home, the morning after the gunshots were fired, my caretaker came to the house grumbling that the elk were eating too much of the hay meant for her horses. She might have to call the sheriff, she said. The hair rose on the back of my neck as I imagined the whine of snowmobiles. Firmly I told her that the sheriff would not be called under any circumstances. We would feed the horses during daylight hours and closer to the house. That should solve the problem. And it did—it was that easy.

Late in the afternoon, I walked up to the barn with the dogs, my pipe, matches, sage for smudging, and a photo of the three elk I had taken weeks before. David had reminded me on my vision quest to call on the spirits of all my relations for help. In Teresa Martino's book *The Wolf, the Woman, the Wilderness*, she wrote that in bygone days the old ones, the wise ones, could become invisible.[1] And so I decided to create my own ceremony, asking Mitaku Oyasin that the elk become invisible to anyone who would harm them.

In the afternoon air, my breath hung like smoke. It was below freezing and would get colder as soon as the sun dropped behind the hills. My hands, bare of gloves, shook with cold. I loaded my pipe with tobacco, put a plug of sage in the bowl, and dusting a cover of snow aside, set the pipe on a log near the side of the barn. Stooping down, I lit a dried twig of sage, blew it out so that the pungent smoke curled up in threadlike tendrils, and moved the photo in and out of the smoke, purifying it. On the hillside to the south, the bull elk rested like three dark comets in the shelter of the aspen trees, watching me. I held up the photo in dying afternoon light and prayed intensely for the elk, asking that the photo represent their physical forms. As I prepared to burn the photo, I prayed that the elk be like smoke to all those who wished them ill, who wished them gone. *Please*, I prayed, *make them invisible*. The tiny flame of the match caught the corner of the photo and set it ablaze. I dropped the handful of flame onto the snow and watched it turn into smoking wafers of black ash. As the smoke faded, I smoked my pipe, offering still more prayers for the safe wintering of the elk and for the safe wintering of all those who lived upon the Earth. *Thank you. Aho, Mitaku Oyasin.*

True to my vision quest, I started a process that winter of slowing down the pace of my life. I was also taking more time each week for some treasured moments and hours of

silent reflection. Both processes were part of my calling to
new beginnings, and both were awakening voices inside me
that were to herald yet another startling and unforeseen
transition in my life.

A week before Christmas, I bolted up in bed in the
middle of the night. A thought hung like a sign printed in fat
capital letters behind my eyeballs: *You will need to sell the house.*
Suddenly I saw the vision of myself in front of a tiny cabin
home—the same vision that had called to me for a brief instant the night of the fire. I left Fritz sleeping in the bedroom, pulled on a thick terry robe, and walked quietly into
the living room. The woodstove still contained a bed of red
coals, and I added two thin logs to rekindle the flame. Arrow
dozed near the sofa, and Strongheart snored on his bed in
the kitchen. The house was quiet, and shadows danced on
the cedar walls as the fire came to life in the stove. Up at the
barn, the horses stood sleeping in the corral. The three elk
rested near the barn door, yellow barn light gleaming off
their antlers and dusting their gray coats with gold. *Sell the
house. How could I?* More realistically how could I not?

My divorce settlement required that I buy Lee's portion
of the house. My mother, who had decided to move closer
to my brother and his wife, also shared equity in the place
and needed her money to move. There are some thoughts
we push away, letting them flutter only along the unat-
tended periphery of our minds. They hover there on the
mental outskirts, struggling to reach us, like the moth that
circles the flame but never quite touches it. Sleep, reflection,
and slow time had brought to me what I refused to admit in
the full light of day: I could not possibly afford to keep the
house after buying out Lee and my mother. The thought
struck me like a hard blow to my stomach, and I doubled

over in shock and pain at the truth of it. I had mistakenly imagined that my new beginnings were about rebuilding the house—not about selling it and moving on to an entirely new life.

After a forest fire, unexpected greenery can suddenly take the place of what was there before, as seeds lying dormant for decades or tens of decades suddenly sprout and change the face of the forest floor. I felt as though I were looking at new flora in my life that I had never seen or planned for. Still, the seeds had been there in quick flashes of a vision of me living a smaller, simpler life—a process I had already begun. The seeds of this new, unexpected beginning had also lodged themselves quietly in my body, fueling my felt sense of being overwhelmed at the magnitude of work needed to maintain the house and land that were mine. I saw the truth of it: the house stood between me and my commitment to simplify and live a smaller life.

The house that had become so much a part of me was another gift I would need to give away. For a long time, I sat and watched the yellow and blue flames dance cheerily in the fireplace as a stream of salt tears coursed quietly down my face. When they had stopped of their own accord, I wiped them away and went back to bed.

The day after New Year's, the first potential buyer—a single woman with a home-based graphic arts business— walked through my house and fell in love with it just as I had the first time I saw it. With no more fuss than that, my home was sold, quickly and irreversibly. Mom, Fritz, the caretaker, and I had three months to vacate and recast new lives for ourselves. A flurry of packing began overnight, and more than ever I came to value the routine and reassuring visits of the elk each evening. Their comings and goings were moments of time in my life that seemed stable and real as winter hurried by, quick as a snowstorm that blows through and out again.

In silence I sat with my pipe by the barn often, asking for guidance. What came to me was a vision of life that was far smaller than I had cast it, lived in smaller space, with a far greater focus on my work. Such a life would mean a far smaller animal family. Trusting in the guidance I'd been given, I began making arrangements for members of my animal family who would not be moving with me. The chickens found a new home with a girlfriend. Polani and Aurora, my precious miniature donkeys, I gave away to a woman who had created a tiny and magical farm-world in a nearby town with llamas, goats, sheep, and a pack of happy, waggle-tail dogs. She sobbed when she came to get the donkey girls, and I did, too—she out of joy, I out of heartbreak.

A year before, I had flown with Pumpkin, my cockatoo, all the way to Michigan to unite her with new people. My travel schedule plus the high, dry mountain air at home were making her depressed and deathly sick. Three weeks later I listened to my sweet bird as her new guardians held the phone up to her beak and she spoke the first new words I'd ever heard out of her. Some animals do better with us, and some without us. Her high-spirited cackle over the telephone lines told me that she was happier in Michigan than she had been able to be with me. I was trusting that the animals I now sent on to new homes would fare as well as Pumpkin, going on to better lives and new soul journeys of their own.

How quickly the three months seemed to race away from me! I got everything ready for moving the dogs and cats, who would be coming with Fritz and me. I had not managed to make any certain plans for my mare, Fashion. I wanted to find a new home for her, wanting as much at the same time to keep her with me. Horse boarding was expensive in my area, and my finances were tight. I didn't see how I could keep her if I didn't have my own property, and I didn't know quite what to do. Then, seemingly out of nowhere, a woman appeared who wanted nothing more than to give a permanent and loving home to my twenty-year-old, slightly arthritic, thoroughbred mare.

Leann Phenix was eager to send out a truck from her home in Austin, Texas, to pick up Fashion. It all happened so fast and fell into place so beautifully that I knew it was the right thing to do. Still, I stalled on Fashion's departure dates. I wanted to keep her as long as I possibly could, to keep alive the memory of the two of us riding in sweet grass and flower-covered pastures that would not be ours for much longer.

Our last month in the house—April—saw the snow leaving in earnest. The three elk began leaving with it, appearing less and less often at the barn. Then they disappeared for two weeks, and I figured they were gone for good, off to their summer feeding grounds in the mountains. Against all odds I had hoped that before they left, one might drop an antler where I could find it. Elk shed their antlers naturally each year around March or April, and an antler from one of my magical elk would have been such a treasure to me. One night a voice in a dream told me that the elk would come back to visit on the full moon and then only a few more times afterward.

The night of the full moon, they did indeed return. Two of them had lost their antlers. The third still had both of his intact. They ate all the hay and grain I had put out in hopes of their coming and slept under the barn light for one more evening. After that I saw them only for brief moments on certain evenings, coming to feed for just an instant, then moving off into the night shadows. Already I was missing them.

Wide patches of wet brown earth began appearing everywhere. The caretaker moved on, taking her horses with her, and Fashion was left alone in the pasture. At night I could hear the drops of snowmelt tinkling off the roof with a sound like a xylophone. Birds flocked to the feeders, chattering loudly. One morning when I went to feed Fashion, I found thin sticks strewn around the barn floor. Looking up, I saw the black, shiny eyes of a magpie looking down at me. The birds had returned to raise another family in the ancient, towering nest. This year I would not be there to see their young grow up.

The house was packed, Mom had moved to her new home next door to my brother, and Fritz and I were set to move into a tiny town house rental on the edge of the highway. I could not afford to buy another home in the area with the money I had left. The town house was the only place we had found that would allow our dogs and cats. My friend Gael asked how I felt about moving into a tiny rental unit with no land around it and the sound of traffic coming at us all day. I told her that it would have to do and that I was grateful to find any place at all to rent that would take animals, especially a dog as huge as Strongheart. "Of course," I added, "my preference would be a small cabin in the woods on the river." We both laughed. River frontage was the land of the multimillion-dollar homes.

One week before we were to close, I arose early and

walked up to the barn through the pastures. The sky was clear, and the sun had not yet come over the hills to spill onto the valley floor. The morning breeze carried the scent of wet ground and last year's yellowed grasses. Fashion followed me up to the corral, and I set a thick pile of hay and a scoop of grain in front of her. While she ate, I took out a bucket of brushes and worked as much of the mud out of her coat as I could. Her winter hair was shedding and fell to the ground around us like brown rain. With my fingers and a thick-tonged comb, I untangled the knots in her mane and tail and wiped the dust away from her nose and eyes. In less than an hour, the truck and trailer would arrive to take her away to Austin and to Leann, who was waiting for her.

I savored the salty scent of my mare, the feel of her, the touch of her velvet lips on my hands and wrists as she searched for the apple treats I always carried. My farm dream had lasted nine sweet years. Life and circumstance were calling me to something else now, though I had no idea what. I would miss dearly the sounds of the barn, of hooves in the straw, and of animals munching hay. I would miss the chore of daily feeding, which took me out into the weather twice each day no matter how soft or hard it was, and the smell of feed and old dust and fresh manure. The barn was a magic place. I had been blessed with two such places to call mine in my life and was grateful beyond measure for them both. Mostly, though, I would miss the presence of the animals themselves: the panache of Polani, the shy delicacy of Aurora, the wise and tranquil elderhood of Fashion.

I heard the sound of tires on gravel and looked up to see a white, shining truck and trailer pull into my driveway.

Slipping Fashion's blue halter over her nose, I stopped to tie the feathers of an eagle and an owl in her hair for protection as she traveled. "Once you were a warrior's horse," I said to her, the words coming from out of nowhere. The green corral gate opened with its characteristic groan, and we walked slowly down to the man who was waiting by the trailer. He was young, burly blond, and dressed in a bright western shirt with a cream-colored Stetson on his head. Eyes to the ground, I handed him Fashion's lead rope, and she stepped into the trailer without looking back. I wanted so much to say good-bye, to put that word out into the morning air, but it stuck in my throat along with the thick wad of tears blooming there, and so I said nothing at all. Our together time was over. Papers changed hands; a few words passed between us. Mine were instructions; his were assurances that he would take special care of my old, noble mare. Leann had seen to that. Then they were gone as I stood waving after them, the sound of tires fading as they turned onto the paved road out front.

A phone was ringing, and I ran up to the barn to grab it, thinking as I picked up the dusty receiver that I had forgotten to pack the thing. It was my friend Sophie, who knew everyone and everything in Jackson Hole. She called to tell me that she had just heard of a tiny old caretaker cabin that had come up for rent on the Snake River. "It's small, and I don't know much about it, but my contractor told me he needed to rent it and soon. I thought of you . . ." I wiped the tears off my face and took down a phone number. When I stepped from the barn, the sunlight had topped the hillside and turned the remaining snow into a sea of white glitter. The sky was as blue as lapis, and the bare aspens reached out their thin, comforting arms to me. Something caught my eye, something resting just under the barn eaves outside near the floodlight. I bent down, eyes wide in gratitude and amazement, and picked up the heavy, earthen-colored antler of a six-point bull elk from where it rested like a thick branch in the snow.

Notes

Introduction

1. Carl Hammerschlag, *The Dancing Healers* (San Francisco: Harper-SanFrancisco, 1998), 12.
2. Gary Zukav, *The Seat of the Soul* (New York: Simon & Schuster, 1990), 31.

Chapter 2: Exile

1. Sy Safransky, "Trail's End," from *Four in the Morning*, excerpted in *The Sacred Earth*, edited by Jason Gardner (Novato, Calif.: New World Library), 20.

Chapter 3: Elk Dreaming

1. Carl Hammerschlag, *The Theft of the Spirit* (New York: Simon & Schuster, 1993), 29.
2. Sun Bear, *Dancing with the Wheel* (New York: Prentice Hall, 1991), xvii.

Chapter 4: Salt Ceremony

1. Renee Beck and Sydney Barbara Metrick, *The Art of Ritual* (Berkeley, Calif.: Celestial Arts, 1990), 5.
2. Carl Hammerschlag, *The Theft of the Spirit* (New York: Simon & Schuster, 1993), 27.
3. Michael Ignatieff, *The Needs of Strangers* (New York: Viking Press, 1985), 29.
4. Quoted in Kent Nerburn, Ph.D., and Louise Mengelkoch, *Native American Wisdom* (Novato, Calif.: New World Library, 1991), 19–20.
5. Sun Bear, *Dancing with the Wheel* (New York: Prentice Hall, 1991), 10.
6. Carl Hammerschlag and Howard Solverman, *Healing Ceremonies* (New York: Berkley Publishing Group, 1997), 8.

Chapter 5: Poison into Good

1. Theodore Roszak, *The Voice of the Earth* (New York: Simon & Schuster, 1992), 56–60.
2. Quoted in Roszak, *Voice of the Earth*, 59.
3. Carl Hammerschlag, *The Theft of the Spirit* (New York: Simon & Schuster, 1993), 105–6.
4. Quoted in Hammerschlag, *Theft of the Spirit*, 109.

Chapter 6: Giveaway

1. Gary Zukav, *The Seat of the Soul* (New York: Simon & Schuster, 1990), 52–53.
2. Teresa Tsimmu Martino, *The Wolf, the Woman, the Wilderness* (Troutdale, Oreg.: NewSage Press, 1997), 73.
3. Carl Hammerschlag, *The Theft of the Spirit* (New York: Simon & Schuster, 1993), 37.
4. Daniel Quinn, *Providence* (New York: Bantam Books, 1995), 166.
5. Christine Davis, *For Every Dog an Angel* (Portland, Oreg.: Lighthearted Press, 1997).

Chapter 7: Refuge

1. Joanne Lauk, *The Voice of the Infinite in the Small* (Mill Spring, N.C.: Swan Raven & Company, 1998).
2. John Neihardt, *Black Elk Speaks* (1932; reprint, Lincoln: University of Nebraska Press, 1998), 194–95.
3. James Lynch, *A Cry Unheard. The Medical Consequences of Loneliness* (Baltimore: Bancroft Press, 2000), 289.
4. Jamie Sams, *The Thirteen Original Clan Mothers* (San Francisco: HarperSanFrancisco, 1994), 55.

Chapter 9: House of My Belonging

1. John O'Donohue, *Eternal Echoes* (New York: HarperCollins, 1999), 2.
2. Ibid., 2–4.
3. C. L. Rawlins, "Grandpa's Horse," in *The Sacred Earth*, edited by Jason Gardner (Novato, Calif.: New World Library, 1998), 118–19.
4. Thomas Moore, "Ecology: Sacred Homecoming," in *The Soul of Nature*, edited by Michael Tobias and Georgianne Cowan (New York: Continuum, 1994), 140.
5. Wendell Berry, "People, Land, and Community," in *Soul of Nature*, 165.
6. Henry Beston, *The Outermost House* (New York: Henry Holt, 1992).
7. Theodore Roszak, *The Voice of the Earth* (New York: Simon & Schuster, 1992), 145.
8. James Lynch, *A Cry Unheard: The Medical Consequences of Loneliness* (Baltimore: Bancroft Press, 2000), 289.
9. Tom Brown Jr., *Grandfather* (New York: Berkley Publishing Group, 1993), 71.
10. Clarissa Pinkola Estes, *Women Who Run with the Wolves* (New York: Ballantine, 1992), 15.
11. J. Krishnamurti, *On Nature and the Environment* (San Francisco: HarperSanFrancisco, 1991), 2.

12. David Suzuki, *Sacred Balance* (Vancouver, B.C.: Greystone Books, 1997), 196.
13. Roszak, *Voice of the Earth*, 145.
14. Annie Dillard, "Pilgrim at Tinker Creek," in *Sacred Earth*, 80.
15. Rachel Carson, "The Sense of Wonder," in *Sacred Earth*, 126.
16. Margot Adler, *Drawing Down the Moon* (Boston: Beacon Press, 1986).

Chapter 10: Leave-taking
1. Doug Boyd, *Rolling Thunder* (New York: Dell Publishing, 1974), 70.

Chapter 11: Intimate Nature
1. Eugene T. Gendlin, Ph.D., *Focusing* (New York: Bantam Books, 1982).
2. Thomas Moore, *SoulMates* (New York: HarperCollins, 1994), 125.
3. Judith Collas, "Change of Life," in *Intimate Nature: The Bond between Women and Animals*, edited by Linda Hogan, Deena Metzger, and Brenda Peterson (New York: Ballantine Books, 1998), 337.
4. Ann Sturgis, letter to the author, July 3, 2001.
5. Ibid.

Chapter 12: Mitaku Oyasin (All My Relations)
1. Teresa Tsimmu Martino, *The Wolf, the Woman, the Wilderness* (Troutdale, Oreg.: NewSage Press, 1998), 104.

A Few Good Resources

The books that appear in the "Notes" section all provided me with a rich storehouse of insight and reflection about animals and the world. I encourage you to read some or all of them.

For readers seeking information on working with animals or animal-assisted therapy, I encourage you to contact Maureen Fredrickson of Animal Systems, at 377 East Main Street, Fredonia, NY 14063, (716) 672-6234, or E-mail her at animalsystems@mindspring.com. She is a wellspring of information and an international expert on these topics as well as on research concerning the health benefits of the human-animal bond.

You may feel a desire to connect with David Bearclaw Abrams about his teachings and ceremonies. He can be reached at P.O. Box 681, Afton, WY 83110.

Any and all other questions you may ever have had about animals and the human condition can be answered by

Best Friends Animal Sanctuary, and I encourage you to get to know this place well. It is a miracle in action. You can reach Best Friends on the Web at www.bestfriends.org, write to them at 5001 Angel Canyon Road, Kanab, UT 84741-5001, or phone them at (435) 644-2001.

ABOUT THE AUTHOR

SUSAN CHERNAK MCELROY is the author of the national best-seller *Animals as Teachers and Healers* and *Animals as Guides for the Soul*. A survivor of advanced cancer, McElroy credits her close relationship with animals as providing the most vital boost toward her healing and recovery. Her award-winning writing appears in numerous anthologies, including the best-seller *Intimate Nature: The Bond between Women and Animals, Kinship with the Animals,* and *Wounded Healers*. She has written for national magazines and is currently working on a series of children's stories. McElroy lectures extensively on the healing bond between humans and animals.

She lives with her animal family in the Rocky Mountain West.

You may write to her in care of Ballantine Books at 1745 Broadway, New York, NY 10019, or reach her through her Web site, www.susanchernakmcelroy.com.